MOTHERS AND DAUGHTERS

MOTHERS AND DAUGHTERS

IRISH SHORT STORIES

Edited by

David Marcus

BLOOMSBURY

First published in Great Britain 1998

This compilation © 1998 by Bloomsbury Publishing Plc

The copyright of the individual contributors
remains with the respective authors

The moral right of the authors has been asserted

Bloomsbury Publishing Plc, 38 Soho Square, London W1V 5DF

A CIP catalogue record for this book
is available from the British Library

ISBN 0 7475 4133 7

10 9 8 7 6 5 4 3 2 1

Typeset by Hewer Text Ltd, Edinburgh
Printed in Great Britain by Clays Ltd, St Ives Plc

Contents

DAVID MARCUS   Introduction   vii

HELEN LUCY BURKE   A Season for Mothers   1

CLARE BOYLAN   The Little Madonna   30

MARY O'DONNELL   Scavengers   41

BERNARD MacLAVERTY   In Bed   51

MARY LELAND   The Little Galloway Girls   60

VAL MULKERNS   Summer   92

MARY BECKETT   Under Control   103

IVY BANNISTER   My Mother's Daughter   116

EDNA O'BRIEN   Cords   124

MARY LAVIN   Senility   140

JULIA O'FAOLAIN   Lots of Ghastlies   163

BRIEGE DUFFAUD   Innocent Bystanders   176

MICHAEL McLAVERTY   Mother and Daughter   201

CAROLINE BLACKWOOD   How You Love Our Lady   213

HARRIET O'CARROLL   Trust   229

LIAM O'FLAHERTY   The Cow's Death   238

Acknowledgements   242

Biographical Notes   245

Introduction

Mother-love is a word you'll find in the dictionary; father-love you won't. A father's love for his children can, of course, be just as intense as a mother's, but one imagines it to be qualitatively different – especially that between father and daughter compared to that between mother and daughter. Presumably that's why I feel myself to be in strange territory in introducing this anthology of Irish short stories about mothers and daughters. Strange, but not alien, for I have a daughter myself.

To observe my wife and our nineteen-year-old daughter colloguing together demonstrates to me that a ghostly umbilical cord not only still joins them, but has become a two-way channel. The variety of themes and tones in the mother-daughter duet played out by the stories in the following pages are natural histories of the hug-and-tug-of-war this human team experiences. Sometimes the stories are hilariously comic, at other times heartbreakingly

INTRODUCTION

tragic, but at all times they are made unforgettable by the
compassion, insight and artistry of some of Ireland's most
celebrated writers. In them mothers and daughters will
recognise some of their own struggles, through them they
will relive many of their supreme joys. Fathers of daughters,
moved by the involuntarily synchronised response of their
own heartbeats, will be enriched by them.

I was.

David Marcus

HELEN LUCY BURKE

A Season for Mothers

S pring brought to Rome the first of the wild asparagus and the baby new potatoes from the South of Italy. It also brought the first and heaviest crop of mothers. Considerable bargaining about them went on between the girls. 'I'll drive yours to Castel Gandolfo if you have mine twice to dinner,' and 'I'm giving a party for mine, and you can bring yours if you introduce mine to the Cardinal.'

Mrs MacMahon arrived by charter-flight at Fiumicino on the Monday after Easter, in all the black glory of her recent widowhood. Martha blinked at the enveloping sootiness, which included a sort of raven's wing attachment on her hat. It was her mother's first visit to Rome, and her first aeroplane trip.

'Never again,' cried Mrs MacMahon. She touched significantly the Rosary beads which hung over her wrist. 'I prayed, and here I am. But never again. Not if I have to spend the rest of my life here.'

'There was a little bit of bumpiness over the Alps, and we all felt it, I'm sure,' interjected an Englishwoman who stood close by. Martha recognised her from previous years as Mrs Whiteside, whose daughter Olive worked with her; they had made a lunch arrangement for their mothers. 'Your mother sat it out in the loo. Only one loo for the whole plane too, dear. Doesn't seem right, does it?'

'What a horrible woman,' said Mrs MacMahon, not waiting until they were out of earshot. 'Common. She told me she had been "in service" if you please. I didn't think that sort of person would be coming out here.' In the car she blinked eagerly at the dry countryside defaced with hoardings, and demanded where St Peter's was.

'There,' said Martha, taking her hand off the steering-wheel and waving it largely at the horizon. Mrs MacMahon immediately crossed herself and bowed her great feathered casque, as would a Moslem towards Mecca. For the rest of the journey she kept turning her head like a compass-needle in the direction Martha had given, while her lips moved. When she suggested going straight to St Peter's to offer thanks for her safe landing, Martha told her it was locked up for the night.

'Locked? Surely not. What about the Monday Night Novena?'

'I don't think there is a Monday Night Novena in Rome.'

Mrs MacMahon set her chin obstinately and informed her that the Holy Father himself had praised Ireland for its devotion to the Mother of God and its attendance at the Novena. 'You just want to keep me away from it, that's all.' In her mind's eye she saw a tall slim figure in white leading the responses, while her own voice joined in, humbly (but audibly), and the tall slim

2

figure in white would become aware of the reverent old Irish voice . . .

Martha's elegant flat received tepid approval.

'Well, you certainly live in style. In style,' nodding a grim condemnatory head. 'Far too grand for the likes of me.' For the latter comment she adopted a meek little voice and sat forward on the edge of her chair, to show that she thought that Martha thought that the furniture was too good for her to sit on. Her temper improved with dinner, which was excellent. She even consented to sip at the chilled Frascati, making wry little mouths to show it was being drunk medicinally, when Martha told her it was the opinion of a Cardinal, whom she would be meeting, that more tourists were killed in Rome by the water than by anything else. There was enough lingering heat in the air to let them step out on the terrace afterwards and identify the huge domes of Maria Maggiore and John Lateran, which heaved themselves out of the jumble of ochre roofs. St Peter's in the far distance was shrouded in mist. Just opposite and below was the modest facade of the local orphanage church.

'I'll get six o'clock mass there tomorrow morning,' said Mrs MacMahon.

'Six o'clock?' cried Martha. 'Couldn't you wait until later?'

But it turned out that later would not be the same at all. In Mrs MacMahon's view Masses fell into the same category as mushrooms and deteriorated as the day went on. 'Just wake me up – you needn't bother to get up yourself. Once I know where it is I can find my own way.' She assumed an air of chivalrous reckless bravery as if Captain Oates were setting out once more into the Antarctic blizzard.

'You know that we have the United Nations Conference for the next ten days,' Martha reminded her. 'You just sit out here on the terrace and take things easy. I'll leave you some money and an Italian phrase-book, and if you like to go shopping there's a good –'

Mrs MacMahon cut her short. 'No! I'm not going to trouble anyone. You won't know I'm here. You'll have your own friends coming here, and what would an old woman do with herself, roasting in the sun at my age, or buying things in the shops to titivate. To pray, that's why I came here. You just drop me at St Peter's on your way to work and collect me in the evenings. I'll be there all day praying. Just praying and thinking.'

Martha's mouth opened and shut again without uttering a sound. It was miles through heavy traffic to St Peter's and more miles in the opposite direction to her office. Besides, it would be as absurd to try and pray in St Peter's as it would be in a railway station. Still, there was nothing for it but to let her mother find these things out for herself. The old lady went to bed, telling Martha not to go to any trouble for her with one of those fol-de-rol continental breakfasts. Just a plain Irish breakfast would do her: fried egg and rasher, and a bit of thin toast. 'None of that pasta for I won't have it.'

'You wouldn't like to just take things easy for tomorrow, and rest yourself after the trip? Cardinal Marconi says more tourists fall ill by overdoing things on their first days than –'

But it turned out that Mrs MacMahon had made a vow, and horrid proof of its potency was provided the following morning when Martha decanted her from the car in the square before St Peter's. Once emerged, she sank first to her knees and then, dreadfully, lay full length on the ground kissing the

4

stones which were wet from the spray of the fountains. 'For his soul, Lord,' she groaned as she reared herself up on her forearms. The posture, combined with her long black dress, gave her the appearance of a seal on a rock. Any idea Martha might have had of escorting her inside and getting her settled, vanished in a twinkling. 'Remember, Lord of mercy, for his sake,' wailed the votary again, sinking down on her flippers, and horrified Martha crying, 'Half-past five at the end of the colonnade' sprang back into the safety of the car. She had provided her mother with 4,000 lire spending money and an Italian phrase-book: what more could she do?

She could have stayed to see me safely into the church, thought Mrs MacMahon. She could have introduced me to the priest in charge. She could have told them I was Irish. She could have taken the day off if she wanted to, and stayed with her mother. From behind the pillars on her right came loud noises of a motor-cycle revving, and the clanking of a tram. She opened her eyes and looked at the pavement from which steam was beginning to rise in little curls as the heat of the sun hit the damp stone. She kissed the hallowed ground, cried out 'For his soul', and marched on the basilica, heavy-footed, awed, reverential, as one of the early Goths.

The air inside struck against her face with the cool dampness of a cave. She noticed a sweetish smell, like an attic with dry-rot. Once more she prostrated herself and kissed, as if it were flesh, the hallowed pavement. St Peter himself had walked here, and St Paul. She planned to visit the church where their dried skulls hung in a basket, as a salutary *memento mori*. What we all come to sooner or later, the worms and the judgment of God before the throne, she had told her husband when he was dying, for he had never been the devout kind that can go with confidence and it was better for him to face up to what must be. His staring terror-filled eyes still troubled her sleep, and called to her for prayers.

'Vietato, vietato,' shouted an Italian voice. A rough hand hauled her from the floor. An official arm waved her on: the other arm gestured at the door behind her where a resentful queue was forming.

'Would you not even leave a widow to her prayers?' she cried at the uniformed back which was hastening in the direction of a group with a movie-camera. 'Oh, great Catholics. Great Catholics indeed, moryah! that don't remember who it is that pays you.'

But sure was it any wonder that they would be lacking in reverence and not a Blessed Martin or an Infant of Prague within sight? No, not a Sacred Heart itself in all the long walk to the top altar, but only a collection of statues which were no fit sight for modest eyes anywhere let alone in a church, and paintings of bold rossies with hardly more than a ribbon to save their decency.

A ballroom is what it is like, she thought. Then she felt guilt for passing such a judgment on the Pope's own church, and for a penance she shuffled to the nearest column which bore an edifying statue. At least the statue had wings and a halo, and it carried a lily in its stony hand, and its dress, though closely fitting enough to show the projection of two large nipples, covered it from throat to ankle. Kneeling, she wondered if it could be the Angel Gabriel, for she had always thought of Gabriel as a male angel; and besides (if he wasn't) he would surely have had the decency to wear a brassière when making the Annunciation.

'For his sake, Lord, and forgive me for criticising Your church.'

When finally she reached the top of the great basilica, she was surprised to find no Mass going on. In her fancy she had imagined the Pope himself at the altar, a Cardinal or two ringing the bells. Even the altar itself was hidden behind a kind of four-poster bed with twisted barley-sugar pillars. But still it *was* St Peter's, the Holy Place, and as she lowered herself again to the marble pavement, making groaning noises like a laden camel, she felt as does a child who has come home. She was at the heart and centre of the mystery.

Worldly and all as some people might think the church, was there not good reason for it? Christ's Vicar on earth must be held in respect by people to whom worldly trappings were all. He himself must think little of it: an austere simple holy man: simple white clothes: the thin nose of him and the bags under his eyes: they couldn't be looking after him properly.

Shifting from one knee to the other she thought of how she would come here day after day, a humble old Irishwoman who trusted in her God, and how the grand people who looked after the church would speak contemptuously of her in their pagan Italian way and laugh at her piety and snigger about her to the Pope. 'We would see her. Take her to Us.' Then the slender white figure raising her from the ground, the dark sad eyes smiling into hers. 'Your faith edifies Us, daughter.' A little conversation then about how she was only a simple Irish widow who had never stirred away from her kitchen until her husband died. 'You can cook, daughter? We have need of you.' An offer of a post as the Papal housekeeper. Feeding him on soda-bread. Once in a while going back to Dublin and paying a smiling visit to Miss O'Toole who was housekeeper to the Parish Priest in Dundrum. Maybe articles about her in the Irish newspapers and about how the Pope was thriving on colcannon and coddle, macaroni quite given up. Nice pots of tea. Potato cakes. 'Then, Miss O'Toole, he looked at me and "Mrs MacMahon" he said, "This is a grand cup of tea," and I said to him, "Holy Father, the secret is to let it draw. Let it draw and warm the pot." So he swallowed a cup of it with a nice hot slice of my soda-cake – I make it with raisins and the bit of butter and the egg – and he said, "Mrs MacMahon, let you give this to Us every morning at 11 and no more of that nasty old macaroni".'

Miss O'Toole barely able to swallow with the bile churning inside her. 'Well, 'tis a fine soft job you have landed for yourself.'

And back I would say, gloated Mrs MacMahon, 'Faith then and it is not, for the devil ever so hard a man on socks you will meet. Sure I'm wore out with the mending of them, and then when himself sees me at them, sure he looks at me with a bit of a smile, the creature, and says the stone floors in the Vatican are very hard on them, and he wearing only the little biteens of red slippers, and the people kissing his foot. No, no,' laughing lightly, 'there's no formality in the family – 'tis what he calls us himself, the family – 'tis just like the man of the house, but holy. Miss O'Toole, the penances that man puts on himself! Amn't I always giving out to him?'

Or would it be more effective to shake her head and purse her lips at enquirers? 'A vow, Miss O'Toole. We all have to make it. The Holy Father wouldn't like us to be blazoning it around what he had for breakfast.' Miss O'Toole would feel the sharpness of that shaft, for she was forever complaining about Father Auger's enormous appetite, but in a proud sort of way like a mother would use in grumbling about a petted son.

The pain in her knees broke in on her daydreams, and when she consulted her watch she was surprised to see that it was only 11 o'clock. The Pope had still not appeared on the high altar to say Mass. There had not even been the flash of a Cardinal's scarlet or the peacock glint of a bishop. At home in Dundrum by this time, she would have taken in three Masses and had an enjoyable gossip with her cronies.

Churches seemed more interesting when there were neighbours to wonder at her sanctity.

'So tell me how you got on?' As she spoke Martha poured two glasses of dry vermouth and added a twist of lemon. It must have been a long day to half-past five for her mother; Martha had found her actually waiting at the colonnade and she had looked tired. 'Where did you have lunch? At that little trattoria I showed you behind the pillars on the right?'

'No,' shrugged Mrs MacMahon, 'I told you many's the time, I'd have nothing to do with that pasta stuff.'

'Sure 'tisn't all pasta. Where did you go, then?'

It turned out that her mother had given the 4,000 lire to a poor priest.

'But there's no such thing,' screamed Martha. 'The fat of the land – a state salary – the Fondo del Culto – my money.'

'It is our duty to give to those in need.' A meek and holy look had made its appearance.

'But your own money, not mine.'

'And was it not mine to buy my lunch? And all I could get with that amount was that pasta. A steak,' she said pathetically, 'or a nice bit of boiled ham, would cost double. The priest I gave the money to told me so. An Irishman he was,' Mrs MacMahon clarified. 'A Maher from Tipperary.'

'Have some more vermouth,' said Martha hopelessly. 'Cardinal Marconi says it's what every pilgrim needs after a day in St Peter's.' She swallowed her own hurriedly and poured herself more. She was going to need it.

'Ordained in Maynooth,' reported her mother the following evening. 'A very good family: they keep horses. His mother was a Nugent from Ballinasloe.' She ate with a good appetite and remarked that she had had no lunch. Martha counted ten.

'Is he long in Rome?'

'I'll tell you tomorrow,' said her mother through a fronded mouthful of spaghetti. (After she had dealt with a large plate of it and two goes of Parmesan cheese, she told Martha that she hated pasta.)

'Three months,' reported her mother on Thursday evening. 'Oh, the poor man. A priest of God. If I told you all I knew –!' She cried a little, then wiping the tears off her cheeks, went on, 'But my lips are sealed. I've given my word and his confidence is safe with me. No!' – raising her hand to still Martha's imagined question – 'you needn't ask. I'll tell you nothing.'

It turned out that he was in trouble with his bishop. 'A Corkman,' said Mrs MacMahon venomously. 'I've never heard good of one yet. But Father Maher will get to the Holy Father in the heel of the hunt, so he will. There's a certain crozier won't be raised high much longer. I'll say no more. I won't be quoted. But you can mark my words, my lady.' A significant smile followed, and a grim shake of the head.

Later they went to a cocktail party given by an Irish diplomat whose sister, Eithne, worked with Martha in the United Nations. His flat was in a tall old building in Trastevere.

'And do you mean to tell me you want your mother – tired and old as she is – to climb those stairs? Oh, it's out of the question.'

'But Cardinal Marconi will be here. He's expecting to meet you.'

'Me?'

'He always meets the mothers.'

'Oh "always" indeed, is it,' said Mrs MacMahon tossing her nose in a dissatisfied way, but making fast for the stairs.

Martha had often met him before: a thin, fly, worldly-looking prelate who frequented diplomatic cocktail parties. He was always ready to meet the mothers of girls in the United Nations. It was a thing understood, but not mentioned, that he was kept supplied with duty-free goods from the staff commissary, for which he usually forgot to pay. It was only for her mother's sake (and to pass an evening) that Martha was attending the party. She had warned her lover, Giorgio, to stay away. She was missing him badly, but he was married and she would not feel easy under her mother's eye.

'Benedico te . . .' intoned the Cardinal over her mother's grizzled head. He helped her to her feet and asked her how she liked Rome, but before she could reply he turned towards the next arrival with real enthusiasm. This was a red-headed girl with a large creamy bust, generously displayed.

Martha urged her mother towards Eithne and the drinks.

'He wants to hear what I think of Rome.'

'Sure can't you tell him later? He has to meet the guests.'

'You mean meet the brazen straps,' said Mrs MacMahon
with a venomous glance at her supplanter. Towards Eithne
she behaved in a queenly manner. 'And where are your
people from? And where did you go to school?' Her eyes
kept straying towards the redhead. 'No brassière on her,' she
whispered to Martha, 'and the tops of her things sticking out
like boils through her blouse. In front of the Cardinal, too.'

'He needn't look at them, sure.'

'Never forget that they are men too. If you were married you
would know what I mean.' She nodded her head portentously,
but with something akin to sympathy for the affliction of a
pair of testicles. Martha was surprised: Rome must be having
a broadening effect. 'And your friend, Eithne or whatever,
is no example either. She certainly can put away the booze.
Must spend a fortune on it. I know the price of it, remember
– ah, who better? Your father . . .'

'Not here you don't. We get it for half nothing at the
commissary. Duty-free and non-profit-making.'

'Ha!' said Mrs MacMahon deeply. 'And people starving.
Starving. Bangladesh. Biafra. Here in Rome, even. The Cardinal
is left on his own.' She made for him with a surprising turn
of speed and left Martha grinning into her drink as she saw
her launch into what she presumed to be a condemnation of
Rome. All the mothers did it. But the Cardinal's experienced
face was growing wary, hunted. He looked furtively around
for succour, smiled supplicatingly at Martha. When in leisurely
pity she drew near she heard him saying, 'But *cara signora*, it is
not so easy. The only time we poor devils of Cardinals see
him is when he wants his triple crown polished.'

They watched him course across the room to the security of Eithne's brother. Mrs MacMahon looked dissatisfied, but all she said was. 'Ve-ry int-er-est-ed was the Cardinal. I'm telling you now, a certain mitre is due for toppling.' After a pause during which she swigged powerfully at her drink, she added, grievedly, 'And I didn't even get a chance to speak to him about your father's soul.'

Getting her out of bed the next morning was a task. After the cocktail party, Eithne had invited them to join her for dinner in a local trattoria. Her brother had come, too, and the red-headed girl with the bosom, and a meek Englishman with a long thin neck whom Eithne was trying to palm off on Martha. Mrs MacMahon had held herself aloof from the food in a severe xenophobic attitude; however, she had allowed her glass to be filled and refilled with the straw-coloured wine from the Castelli. Martha had had to undress her and put her to bed, while she talked of repentance and the sufferings of the Saviour.

'I have to go now. The Conference will be under way.' She looked uneasily at the old lady, whose face was leaden under two gay rosettes of rouge. 'Would you not do better to rest at home today? The day after tomorrow is Sunday and we'll be going to St Peter's to get the Pope's blessing. In the meantime —'

'For your father's soul. A vow is sacred.' The old lips clamped together in a pleated mauve line of determination. 'I've made a promise.'

Yes, but what and to whom, Martha wondered. Her mother was carrying a bucket-bag which made a clinking sound of glass, and she had a presentiment that if she went to her drinks cupboard some of the Irish whiskey would be gone. Better to

13

keep quiet about it. Her mother probably wanted an Elizabeth of Hungary situation, illicit alms turning into roses.

During the night a fine rain had fallen. It left a polish of damp on the stones of the square. The car-wheels skidded as Martha roared away, already late for the Conference. Half-way down the Via della Conciliazione however, she stopped the car, prompted by worry for an old woman in the grip of her first hangover. The small black figure was toiling across the immense space between the enfolding claws of the colonnade. One of her shoulders was dipping from the weight of the bucket-bag. 'Christ! she must have taken the whole four,' Martha said aloud.

It could have been worse. During the day the girls with visiting mothers compared notes. Freda Livingstone's sat all day in the entrance lobby, knitting a brown garment which was thought to be a Franciscan shroud. Letitia's had struck an Italian with a bottle in some obscure quarrel about cruelty to a cat.

'No-one before has ever had a mother in Rebibbia prison. What shall I do? What shall I do?'

'The Lord save us, prison's nothing these days. Why should you be worrying about prison?' urged the Irish girls. But Letitia was English and respectable and would not be comforted.

'Mine has to have gruel in bed at night,' contributed Catherine Kelly. 'I had to buy oats from a stable at the race-track and grind them in my coffee-mill.'

In the face of other people's trials Martha felt a little happier. That evening however, for the first time, her mother was not waiting for her. She appeared finally, after about half an hour, walking with tottering steps from the wrong direction. The bucket-bag swung lightly but her shoulders were bowed.

Alarmed, Martha helped her into the car. Once inside, a strong smell of alcohol made itself felt. Grappa, and raw ignorant grappa at that. Hair of the dog. Oh dear.

They were in the thick of the Friday evening rush. Cars dashed vehemently across slippy intersections, trumpeting their anger at each other. As they turned up the green slope of the Aventine Hill the drizzle quickened in tempo; rain bounced back off the ground with a roaring noise. The film of oil on the cobbles made the car-wheels spin to the side, as horses' hooves might long ago have slipped and grabbed. It gave Martha an excuse to slow down to a crawl as she came near Giorgio's place, for she could see his pearl-grey outline, as he sat in his car. He stared with unconcealed interest at her mother, but made no sign, and she drove on. Giorgio was always cautious.

'Horrible staring oily people. Can't you be going on?' groaned Mrs MacMahon. 'The light is hurting your mother's eyes. I don't care for this place at all. Pagans in palaces, that's what they are.' Lost on her was the gracious beauty of the villas set back amid lush gardens, where Horace and Lucullus would have felt at home; lost was the Byzantine splendour of the Aventine churches, and the paved square, with its perfection of carving around the gate to the garden of vines. All, all was alien: the stones, the strange historic hills, the olive staring faces, the ochre of the peeling buildings, even the quality of the light, for in the evening Rome was illumined from the West with a mirror reflection from the sea, which now glared slanting through the deluge. When she moaned 'The light, light' she was mourning the dying of the sun against a moist Northern plain, and the gentleness of a city where sun and rain were benefactors, not tyrants. But she had fled to this place to escape the silence of her own house, and the cold bed whose springs were still dented by the shape of her husband.

Martha, making an effort to know all and to forgive all, could feel only an ache in her bone for Giorgio's touch and resentment that her mother's presence made meetings impossible. She wished she knew when her mother's air-ticket expired. A fortnight she could take – maybe three weeks. How long would Giorgio wait?

'I met Maura Cregg and I arriving at the airport.' An onslaught was preparing, for as she spoke Mrs MacMahon was striking the palms of her hands together.

'Did you.' Flat. Uninterrogative.

'A class behind you at school, wasn't she?'

'Before me.'

'Just the year anyway. The one year.' From the corner of her eye Martha could see her mother's head nod meaningly. As no comment came back, she had to proceed unprompted. 'Nine children she has, and a tenth on the way.'

'Disgusting,' said Martha. 'Having them in litters like a rabbit or a guinea-pig.'

'Ha, my lady, you wouldn't say that if they were your own,' cried her mother in a triumphant tone. 'That's what makes the difference – when they're your own.'

'If they look anything like her, they must be a grim collection.'

'She got her man, anyway, didn't she? Buck-teeth and all, she got her man.' There was a respite while Mrs MacMahon mused on the scalp tucked into Maura Cregg's belt, which conferred a superior status on her mother, old Mrs Cregg. Martha would have been astonished had she heard her own mother's version of Martha's spinsterhood – the offers she had turned down, the Roman princes and bishops' nephews begging for her hand, and all turned down in favour of a career.

'And does the car and the flat really make up for everything?' she asked suddenly.

'I work for them,' Martha replied obliquely. She knew that what appeared to be a question was really a statement: that she was being condemned for living an empty frivolous luxurious life in a foreign capital, instead of the penitential meritorious life of an Irish wife and mother.

'Horrible people,' tittered her mother, peering through the misted window at two lorry-drivers abusing each other.

'Cardinal Marconi says anything south of Florence is mission territory, with cannibals.'

'Not much I would think of him, to be abusing his own. Cardinal Macaroni we call him.'

Ha! We! thought Martha, disgusted. She changed the subject. 'I don't have to work tomorrow so we can sleep on. I'll take you to the square on Sunday morning to see the Pope. 'Twas unlucky that the Conference was on.'

'But you'll drive me to St Peter's in the morning!' It was a frantic statement, not a request or a query.

When Martha said she needed to lie on and unwind, perhaps might bring her on a little stroll around the tombs of the Scipios in the afternoon and go to Nemi or Tivoli on Sunday afternoon, Mrs MacMahon became incoherent with anxiety, which lasted through dinner. She passed from this into rage, and after a lengthy period of haranguing, into loud recriminations when Martha went into her own room and locked the door behind her. 'I thought this was to be my holiday,' came the voice through the keyhole. 'What would

I be wanting with your tombs?' A Conference, indeed! How well she knew that Martha could get away from it easily if she wanted. And then when her mother went back she would tell everyone how good she had been to her, the trouble she had gone to, the expense it had been.

It had been Mrs MacMahon's secret intention to end her days in the Holy City. She had thought that her years of prayer and Mass-going had given her a lien on the Church of Rome, as if she would be coming to the house of her close kindred. Instead she found herself in a vast unfriendly museum, with paid attendants instead of the saintly clergy she had expected. The authority which she had expected to wield over Martha was become a weapon in Martha's hand, under Martha's roof and eating her food. And though Martha was being ostentatiously kind, she made it plain that it would last for a set term of weeks. The thought of returning to the silent house in Dublin made Mrs MacMahon sick with terror, but Rome held no refuge. She was treated as an aged child with holiday whims to be gratified, and she knew (for she had overheard a phone-call) that her foibles were discussed and exchanged against the rival foibles of other visiting mothers. She was presented to a Cardinal as if he were something rare and diverting that would soothe a fractious toddler, and she was supposed not to notice but to be grateful to her daughter.

There was also the question of Martha's almost sinfully luxurious style of living, with a car as long and glittering as a railway train, and the way she was turning into an old maid, fussing about cigarette burns on the furniture, needing everything about her meticulous, so that the next thing would be a cat. She bent and shouted through the keyhole, 'A dried-up old maid.'

In the morning Martha lay in bed and listened to tinklings as her mother grappled with the phone-system. Later, they met coldly and enquired how each other had slept. Mrs MacMahon had a furtive look on her face: checking her cupboard, Martha found a box of 500 cigarettes missing.

Saturday was a day of armed truce and scant words. Only on Sunday as they drove towards St Peter's did Mrs MacMahon relax again into her accustomed tone of command, with admonitions to hurry. And then when they got to the square it was very little different from its weekday self. 'You mean he appears for the blessing, and the Romans know it and still don't come?' she cried, incredulous at the sparse huddled knots of foreigners. Her eyes were anxious, straining right and left obviously for some rendezvous.

Martha saw him first and recognised him out of the foreboding of her heart. He wore a black polo-neck sweater to hide the seediness of his Roman collar; his shoes were unpolished, which marked him out in that city of spruce princelings; about his clothes was that greasy look of the drinking civil-servant or the drinking priest. But his face was not bad, she conceded; no better than she had expected. A sort of ruined boyishness and vulnerability.

'Why, if it isn't Father Maher!' cried her mother. 'If it isn't yourself!'

He acknowledged the greeting with a small anxious smile, and turned to Martha for the introduction. His blue eyes held apology and appeal. Martha might have softened if she had not known that it was her own whiskey which twitched in his hands and reached her in a powerful waft of alcohol and peppermint.

'And so few people,' her mother went on busily. 'I declare

19

to God 'tis a scandal. If 'twas in Dublin he lived, the crowds would come, faith.'

'The Italians aren't much,' said Father Maher. He coughed and looked nervously at Martha.

'That's what I'm tired telling her, but she knows better than her mother. Oh they all do, these days. Nothing but Rome and the Italians will do my lady here.'

'Most of my friends are Irish or English,' said Martha mildly.

'And Italian Cardinals,' laughed her mother with a wrinkling of her nose. 'Oh yes, the Italian Cardinals. Cardinal Macaroni, no less,' she nodded to Father Maher.

At this point the Pope appeared on his balcony and the subject was dropped, but as they fell to their knees for his blessing, Martha saw a parcel and an envelope change hands. There go my brandy and my cigarettes, she thought, and my money too as sure as eggs. She stole a look at her mother who was sunk on the stones in an ecstasy of religion. She had joined her hands high and held them in front of her pointed at the balcony, while her eyes sighted along them as along the barrel of a rifle, at the mournful face with the large crooked nose and the black eyes and the obstinate complacent mouth, which embodied for her the living representative of Christ.

'He doesn't look as if he gets enough to eat, the poor Pope; that pasta couldn't be agreeing with him. Nasty greasy stuff it is too, that must incline his skin to pimples.'

'Ah, sure if you're hungry you'll eat anything,' said Father Maher.

'A life of penance,' agreed Mrs MacMahon. 'And sure I suppose yourself, in the excitement, came out without any breakfast?'

They turned confident pre-arranged faces to Martha. As she weakly gestured them into the car she saw little conspiratorial smiles exchanged. It was blackmail, simply blackmail.

'Let Father Maher drive,' Martha heard, and heard Father Maher magnanimously refuse. Oh, Ireland was the home of the priest, all right, where they could reign Turk-like over their seraglios. When she heard her mother pipe, 'Not too fast, now; Father Maher doesn't like going too fast,' she put her foot hard on the accelerator. At wicked speed they drove through the dusty outskirts of Rome, through the crowded country villages at the foot of the hills, along a road that nudged past lakes with antique names, towards the green mountain of Nemi where once the murderers had taken refuge in the Golden Grove.

Showing some fineness of spirit Father Maher kept up a jerky and one-sided conversation. Sunday customs in Italy. Officially Catholics. No true devotion. Admirable family spirit though too inclined (little cough) to the flesh. Italian driving. Opera. The food. And Mrs MacMahon, who had seen a magical sign indicating 'Castel Gandolfo, Palace of Pope', abandoned her ritual cries of fear and lost herself in imaginings of how she, a poor Irish widow, would get to the Pope and reveal the injustices perpetrated by his underlings. 'Mrs MacMahon. We knew nothing of this. Our subordinates have betrayed Our trust.' 'Poor priests driven into a state of nerves and terror by these bishops. Corkmen, they are the worst.' 'Daughter, you have Our ear. Speak in confidence.' All she needed to get to the Pope was someone with a little bit of influence who spoke Italian. Her daughter, now, would be the one to do it if she wanted to oblige her old mother. Had there been something odd in the way Cardinal Marconi had made himself scarce, and he so obviously well-known to Martha? Was it possible that she had turned the Cardinal against Father Maher out of jealousy? Huddled into a bundle she brooded on the brightness of the life she would have had, if only she had been blessed with a son like Father Maher. There would be first Masses and first blessings and anointed young male hands laid gently on the old grey head, not to speak of the admiration of all her butties who had to make do with being priests' housekeepers, having been left old maids on the shelf.

They had turned off the main road and looped up the mountain under a canopy of lime and pine. Martha caught sight of her mother's face in the rear mirror: it was tense, absorbed. Her hands were clenched and working. It is because she is at the end of her life, thought Martha, and has nothing to hope for. She must feel necessary to something, even if it is only to a leech. Once more she made the resolution that understanding all she would forgive all. Her mother would not have much longer in Rome. She would make this lunch a memorable one.

She had arranged to meet Olive and her mother, the jolly ex-cook Mrs Whiteside, with whom Mrs MacMahon had travelled. It was an unpropitious appointment but one which Martha had to keep, for she was under a few obligations to Olive in matters relating to her affair with Giorgio: messages had been passed on during difficult times. And after all, she reflected, in the exquisite surroundings of Nemi, who could feel anything but peace and goodwill? She parked the car beside the wall of the great towering castle, and they walked over the polished cobblestones of the square, dappled with small flying shadows as the swallows, crying in thin voices, dipped and wheeled against the sun, to where Baffone's restaurant clung to the edge of the cliff, a thousand dizzy feet above the lake.

The two Whitesides were sitting at a table under the trellis, in the young warmth of the Spring sun. As she approached, Martha saw them mutter to each other and gape. Their nods to Father Maher were barely perceptible, a minimum lowering of two sets of double chins, at which he seemed to shrink into himself and grow smaller.

Over the aperitifs the mothers eyed each other with the doubtful eye and bristling neck of dogs making up their minds to fight. Mrs Whiteside had been in Rome a number of times before, and she took it on herself to patronise Mrs MacMahon. 'What! haven't seen the Trevi Fountain yet, dear, or the Spanish Steps? Missing a lot, dear, aren't you?'

Mrs MacMahon fought back creditably, her ground being that as a Catholic she was in the deepest sense a native of Rome.

'You wouldn't understand what we feel, Mrs Whiteside. The sense of homecoming.'

'Oh yes, and with the Father to show you round, no doubt.' There was an unpleasant shade of meaning in her glance. Father Maher muttered something about not being very familiar with the place himself. 'Oh, yes, the Vatican and St Peter's,' pursued Mrs Whiteside. 'You would know. Practically your own firm, I mean.'

The waiter arrived with another round of drinks, which were paid for by Martha although they had been silently signalled for by Father Maher. Mrs MacMahon, accepting hers, made the waiter a queenly gesture to keep Martha's change, and then, reversing roles, made democratic little remarks about Mrs Whiteside's former life in service, and what a relief it must be now for her to sit back and let other people do the fetching and carrying. She urged her not to be a bit ashamed of her occupation. 'No shame at all in any kind of honest work, so long as it is done for the love of God. Housework or kitchen work or anything. I never treated my maids as anything less than the family, and I trained Martha the same way. It all depends after all on the position God has allotted us. NO SHAME AT ALL,' in a loud slow voice, fixing Mrs Whiteside's eyes with her own and slightly extending her hand as if she were raising her from the slime. 'Remember that Christ called His apostles from the humblest fishermen.'

'You do take things seriously. Laugh, that's my motto.' Mrs Whiteside wheezed out a jolly sound, but her eyes were cold and wicked like pickled onions. She proceeded to tell far from Christ-like stories about life below stairs.

Mrs MacMahon bowed her head and puckered her lips as if she were sucking a private slice of lemon. The hunch of her shoulders showed her suffering in sympathy with Father Maher, whose mother had been a Nugent of Ballinasloe. At a gap in the stream of narrative she interjected, 'And do you mean to tell me, Mrs Whiteside, that you, a Christian, come to the Holy City without trying to set eyes on our Holy Father? Fountains and restaurants, is that all it means to you?'

'I saw him all right,' said Mrs Whiteside testily. 'Looks as if he suffered from his kidneys, doesn't he, with those yellow circles under his eyes. Up all night running, I wouldn't doubt.'

'A saint,' said Mrs MacMahon. 'I saw him this morning. This very morning.'

'So did we see him this morning. Saw you, too, we did, and the Father, di'n't we, Olive?' She laughed in a significant

24

way and fished a cherry out of her drink. Smiling down at it, she said, 'Oh yes. Our second time to meet the Father, i'n't it, Olive? Not that he remembers, I'll be bound.'

'Cigarettes,' said Father Maher. He looked around vaguely, and then walked off across the piazza.

'Call the waiter for him, can't you, Martha,' cried tender Mrs MacMahon.

'The widow's Curse,' Olive contributed. She too laughed.

'The what? What do you mean?'

'That's what they call him. Came round trying to get money from me in St Peter's last week. Go away, I said, you'll get nothing from me. My house is a house of prayer, I said, and I'll call those Swiss in their uniforms and see what they have to say. Smelling of drink – disgraceful I call it.'

'Lucky we saw you to warn you,' said Olive. 'That's what Mum said to me. Here, she said, we'll have to warn the MacMahons, didn't you, Mum? But then you slipped away.'

'Gave us quite a turn to see you walking over with him. Tries all the women on their own, he does. Teaches you, doesn't it?'

'And one thing it doesn't seem to have taught you is charity,' said Mrs MacMahon in a trembling voice. 'Judge not that ye may not be judged.'

Mrs Whiteside ate her cherry in a considering way. 'Oh I don't know, I'm sure. Not that I'm judging. Think about these things differently in Ireland, don't you? Probably seems quite normal to you.'

'And if a poor priest drinks too much occasionally, isn't it a disease? Who and what drives him to it?'

'Oliver Cromwell, I suppose. All you Irish are the same, anyway.'

25

All pretence of a social neutrality had been abandoned. The two mothers, their faces congested, leaned across the table, only separated from blows by its fortunate width. Martha, cringing, looked furtively around at the other tables where three generations of happy Italian families guzzled. Loud voices at least would not be remarkable, but Giorgio sometimes brought his family to this restaurant.

'And after 700 years of tyranny by England is it any wonder? Plundered and oppressed. It's a wonder itself that you're not ashamed to look an Irish person in the face.'

'Oh I don't know, I'm sure,' said Mrs Whiteside, dealing with another cherry. Through the masticated pieces she added, 'Seems to me anything Oliver Cromwell did, you've done worse in England. Drinking all day long on Social Welfare. Going home at night to have more children at our expense. Fights all the time, drink, and the priests as bad as any, I ask you.'

'And what about that English clergyman, so-called, at Castle Sant' Angelo last week? Over all the papers in Rome. With young boys. A sin that I didn't even know existed until here. Martha read it all out to me. Faugh!' – tossing her head about and stretching her neck as if she were about to be sick – '*We* keep ourselves clean. Natural.'

'Ho, natural indeed,' shrilled Mrs Whiteside. 'Nice natural daughter you have too.' Martha felt an intense pain in her ankle as Olive's foot, lashing towards Mrs Whiteside, missed its target. 'Ask her how she got her promotion. Ask her how she runs her big car and gets all the time off.'

'How dare you? Liars, all the English.'

'Liars? Made off quick enough, your priest did. Drunken Irish. You ask your daughter –'

'And you ask yours what she said to the whole office about her mother the ex-cook. The way she is ashamed to have you here with your dirty stories.'

'Liar,' panted Mrs Whiteside. 'My Olive is a fine girl.'

'No maid-servant is going to say anything in front of me about Martha that was reared in a decent Irish home, far from the likes of ye.'

Neither Martha nor Olive looked at each other as they led away the aged gladiators in opposite directions. It was the kind of thing that always happened in the mothers' season.

'Sinful slanderous lies.'

Martha agreed.

'First on to the poor priest that she thought had no-one to defend him. Then as if that was not enough, on to you.'

'Appalling.'

'As if,' said Mrs MacMahon, 'I would believe what she said about you, and she after taking the character of Father Maher. We're better off without her and her snib of a daughter. Supposing Cardinal Marconi had seen us with the likes of them, what would he think? A cook, by your good leave. We'll have lunch instead in that nice town of the Pope's we passed on the way up.'

'Castel Gandolfo,' said Martha hopelessly. Father Maher's seedy black figure was leaning against the bonnet of her white car, like something symbolic. Even at that distance she could detect the timid ingratiating smile.

'Father Maher knew how to deal with them. Just up, and quietly left them to it. I feel ashamed of myself for exposing him to people like that. His mother was a Nugent of Ballinasloe, too, you know.'

By this they were close enough for him to see the victory

flush and the conquering tilt of the black-winged Viking hat. His own outline seemed to swell in sympathetic relief.

'We've had enough of that lot,' explained Mrs MacMahon. She climbed grunting into the rear seat.

'My mother fancies lunch in Castel Gandolfo.'

'If that's all right with you, Father,' cried the anxious voice from behind.

Father Maher nodded his agreement.

'We might meet someone useful – Cardinal Macaroni, maybe. Or the Pope might be spending the afternoon there.'

Another nod from the clerical incubus.

'You must be tired,' solicitously. 'That little tiny airless room of yours you told me about – sure you could never get a decent night's sleep.'

They had just turned downhill from the town, into an alley of budding limes which cut off the sunlight, and Martha felt a simultaneous access of cold to her heart. She knew what her mother was planning. And all her life her mother had won. Not one but two Old Men of the Sea were planning to mount on her back. Where would Giorgio fit in? Except in the office they had had no contact since her mother arrived, and already he was becoming impatient. It was not the passionate impatience of a Romeo, but the tetchy impatience of someone kept waiting in a supermarket.

'Do you know,' said her mother, thrusting her great black hat between the priest and Martha, 'I had been dreading the journey home in the plane, back to the empty house, and sure I think Martha, the poor creature, wasn't looking forward either to being left on her own, for all that we've had our little differences. Martha sees now that her mother was right, for all that I've never been out of Ireland before. Faith, Martha walked off on them quick enough, that vulgar pair, when they started in on Ireland and the clergy. And on her mother, on her mother. For all she's been living in Rome, Martha's Irish.'

The hat was withdrawn. Two thuds indicated shoes kicked off. After a long musing pause Mrs MacMahon added in a cosy tone. 'Sure it just goes to show you, that the Irish never appreciate each other, until we encounter the foreigners, the Italians and the English.'

CLARE BOYLAN

The Little Madonna

Look at this. I found it in *The Sun*. It's about a sixteen-year-old called Dolores and her three-month-old daughter, Marigold. 'The Little Madonna', they called her. She has a perfect heart-shaped face and rosebud lips that curve up into a sweet smile. The baby's face was a miniature heart with the same rosebud. Dolores had no job and no one to support her. She was given a council flat. People brought her money and food. Everybody looked forward to seeing her out with the baby, her hair neatly tied in a bunch on top of her head, the baby's scraps of fluff tied up in imitation. Dolores wore a long Indian caftan and the baby had a little Indian smock over her pram suit. People agreed it made you think the world wasn't so bad when you saw them out together. A Mr Cecil Dodd, who owned the shop across the road, said it changed your mind about the female sex.

One day the Little Madonna put the baby out in the playground in her pram because she wanted to take a rest.

It was Mr Dodd, rubbing a clear patch on his shop window, wondering if the papers would be delivered on such a day, who saw a ghostly hump beyond the railings of the flats. The pram was completely covered in snow and although his heart hit off his rib cage when he sprinted out to see, he told himself it was only foolishness, no one would put a child out on such a day.

'There!' he reassured himself when he reached the pram for there was only a toy – a little white woolly bear. It looked so cold he had to touch it and his finger traced beneath the rasping surface, a small, cold slab of forehead, a heart-shaped face, milky blue. His first thought was to wonder who had done it and what they had done to Dolores. He banged on her door, but it was open. She was lying on the floor, near a radiator. He knelt beside her and stroked her face. She opened her lovely gentle eyes: 'I was having a sleep. It was cold so I lay down by the radiator.'

'The baby . . . !' he said.

'It's all right,' Dolores smiled. 'She didn't suffer. I read that people who freeze to death just get very sleepy and then drift off with no pain. I was very careful about that.'

Mr Dodd told this story in court, in support of Dolores's character, even though the inquest had revealed a dappling of long, plum-coloured bruises underneath the little Indian shirt.

The report in *The Sun* is more economical. You have to read between the lines. 'Baby Freezes while Mum Snoozes,' it says. Had the baby failed to freeze to death, she would have been a Miracle Baby, but that is beside the point.

I have this propped up against the milk jug while I'm eating my breakfast. I'm trying to work it out. Who would leave a sixteen-year-old to look after a baby? I remember Rory, who was a good child and sensible, relatively, cut her wrists very neatly with a razor blade when she was sixteen. Being an intelligent girl she read up some books first to make sure the slits would not go through, but it was a very bad moment for me and she meant it to be.

I am not young. I'm a has-been. I'm on the heap and let me tell you this, it's quite a comfortable place to be. When my womb packed up I went through a sort of widowhood although my husband was not yet dead. I went around sighing, drinking cups of tea to wash down the nerve-stunning pills I bought from a doctor. For a mother to learn that she can have no more children is for a surgeon to have his hands cut off. What can she do? You can't make the children you have last indefinitely. After a long time it came to me that the void was not in my stomach at all. It was in my head. The womb does not have a brain, but that is like saying that the rat is not an intelligent creature. It comes programmed with the cunning of survival. When a young girl presents herself and her head full of dreams to her lover it is natural for the womb to say, 'Let me do the thinking, dear. You just use your pretty head for painting your pretty face.' That's how it is. No, excuse me. That's how it was.

This emptiness I located in my head was not new. It had been there since I was a young woman, Rory's age. My hands were full and my lap. I used my intelligence as a rat does, to plot a path through the maze. Now that the high walls of the maze had crumbled I found myself in open fields. Thoughts rose up into my head. I realised that the period of mourning which succeeds the menopause is not a grieving. It is the weariness that follows upon the removal of a tyranny. Now

I was free. I made up my mind never to cook again and became an enthusiastic collector of complete meals in plastic bags with added vitamins. I began, recklessly, to allow entry to thoughts that were not my immediate concern – none of my business at all, to be perfectly frank.

I gave up *The Guardian* which was still telling me how to raise my children and my political consciousness. I started buying *The Sun* which told me about homicides and sex scandals and the secret vices of the royals and reminded me how bountiful women's breasts were. It was the start of my expanded thinking. Every day I find a new marvel on which to ponder.

Why, I ask myself this morning, would anyone leave a sixteen-year-old in charge of a baby? What about all those people who said they brought gifts of food? Why didn't they sneak inside and offer to change the baby's nappy to see if it was being fed all right or if it was being beaten? Who would leave a baby with a sixteen-year-old?

And it comes to me, quite suddenly, sprouting out of the scrap-heap of my middle-aged head – God did. God the Father! He gave His only son to a girl of fifteen. There, with my cup of tea in one hand and my fag in the other, I am filled with alarm as if there is something I should instantly do. I can see the baby with his nappy on backwards as his mother puts henna in her hair. He's crawling around on his hands and knees in his father's carpentry shop, his little mouth full of nails, waiting with growing hopelessness for his mother to come and make him spit them out. Oh, God.

Now there's a thing just caught my eye. 'Orgy and Bess' is the heading. It's about an heiress, Bess Hichleigh-Harrow, who is alleged to have offered the sum of £10,000 to any man who could make her experience an orgasm. She looks a nice ordinary woman. Her coat is good.

There is a great preoccupation with orgasms in the modern world, their frequency, their intensity, their duration. Why choose a muscular spasm as an obsession and not something full of mystery, like a bat or a bee? Why not blame the orange for failing to make us happy and fulfilled?

Because it comes to us from our lover, our husband, our mate, our enemy, with whom all things become possible – whose fault everything is.

Of all the things that rose up in my mind after my womb folded up, orgasms wasn't one. I thought of Rory's bottom, when she was a baby – that hot, clothy acquiescence, serene as a Rajah on its throne, pissing indifferently over her legs and my arms while her own arms, entirely dignified and intelligent, patted my face.

She came in the morning. I called her Aurora – a rosy dawn. I was flabbergasted. At long last, after all the false promises, the beloved had come and she came from myself who, being young, I also loved. Men marvel at rockets to the moon and are not astounded by the journey of a sperm to the womb, the transformation of liquid into life. Only women are amazed. 'I'm not pregnant, not me, I can't be!' they tell the doctor. 'Why me?' they rail at God, and are further dismayed when the emergent infant shows no gratitude to its host, but shits and spits and screams like the devil.

Rory was not like that. She loved me, not just in the way little girls love their mothers, but with the deep earnest love that some men have for their wives, which also contains a small element of contempt. Unlike other children she respected me as the bearer of her life but she thought of me as a simple, shallow person, out of touch with reality. I tried to get myself in shape. I read Freud and Kate Millet and Carl Jung and The Guardian. It wasn't easy keeping up. Rory grew up in the seventies when everything happened.

I was full of curiosity about the new woman; to be free of priests, to see the penis as a toy, to open one's body to men and lock the door of the womb. 'Tell me,' I coaxed her. Do you know what she told me?

'You were lovely,' she said, 'before Daddy died. Why did you have to change?' My generation were the essential women. We were structured to our role and submitted without grievance. That's what she said. We gave birth in our season without ever giving it a thought. That's what she thinks.

She remembered me in a flowered apron and high-heeled shoes, dabbing on my powder – slap, slap, slap – so that it sat on my nose in a comfortable, dusty way, like icing on a bun. A bright, dry, crimson lip was put on, like a felt cut-out and then blotted on to the lower lip and then the glorious gold compact with its wavy edges was snapped shut with a sophisticated clack, and slipped into a little black bag.

'Remember?' she said. There were tears in her eyes.

Rory comes to visit me once a week although she is not comfortable in the heartless flat I bought after her father died. I hide The Sun under a cushion, but she finds it. 'What can you be thinking of?' she asks in exasperation.

She is thirty-two. There are lines around the edges of her eyes and her jaw is starting to set, which is an unnerving thing to see on your own child. So I tell her: 'I was thinking of the Virgin Mary!' I light a cigarette but I have to hold it away at an angle because she doesn't like the smoke.

I suppose the point of it all was that she was only fifteen.

Who else could an angel of the Lord have declared unto? I wonder now, why people make such a fuss about the virgin birth? As if making love had anything to do with having babies. What do you suppose she said to her mother and father afterwards? 'I'm going to be the mother of God!'? 'I'm pregnant!'?

'I saw an angel'. I'll bet that's what she said. Afterwards, when she remembered, she told them what the angel said, that like any old mother everywhere, she had conceived of the Lord.

What on earth did her mother say, her good Jewish mother from the house of David who had gone to such trouble to make a nice match for the child? Don't tell me she took it on the chin. An easy lay and a liar, yet! She was too old to have her daughter's faith, but if she had, she would have asked: 'What was its wing span?'

'Look at this!' Now that Rory has pulled my Sun out from under its cushion the gloves are off. ' "Bag Baby Found in Bin"!'

This is my favourite story today. It's about Norman who was found in a bag which was then stuffed down into a bin. It is a large denim shoulder bag, well enough worn to be prudently discarded. Baby Norman seemed to accept this as his world, or hiding place, and was angry only when disturbed. He has a very red face with rough patches like a butcher's hands. He is not winsome. The item is an appeal for his mother to come back and claim him but his mother has ditched dour Norman, she has sacrificed her battered denim shoulder bag which she probably quite liked, and callously pinned the name 'Norman' on his little vest. She has put the tin lid on him and she is never coming back.

Now I've made my daughter miserable. She says I am growing morbid. As you grow older you see things differently. Cause, you realise, is only the kite tail of effect and God is a lateral thinker. I heard a Chinese fable once which said that fate bestows a gift for life on every child at birth. Perhaps Baby Norman's gift was to be left in a bag. Someday, when he is an ugly man being reviled by a woman, he will tell her that his mother left him in a bag in a bin, and her heart will break and she will take him on. He would have been ugly with or without his mother's indifference, but who else would have loved him if his mother had? Rory says you can't believe anything you read in *The Sun*. I suppose she's right, yet she believes absolutely and without a wisp of doubt that Mr Gorbachev is ready to lay down all his arms.

There is only one mystery left in life, or at any rate in the Western world, where people have opened out the brain and the soul, analysed the body's responses and claimed for themselves in everything from work to love to life or death, the right to choose. Only the child remains the unchosen one. Who knows whether twin soul or tyrant comes dimpling from the neck of the cervix? Cells gather inside us in secret like a pack of dogs or a flock of angels. It could be the Messiah. It could be the man in the moon. Only a child would open Pandora's Box.

Only a Marigold or little Norman's mother would have the nerve to shut it again.

Rory is right. I was lovely before. I made lemon drops and shepherd's pies and fairy cakes. Women play house to preserve a moment that once was almost theirs, the same way they paint their faces to hold youth a little longer. My husband used to tell me – or tried to tell me – over and over, about a trip in a canoe with his father when he was seven. That's all I remember except for official reports issued daily over the tea table. For all I knew about him he might have been a fish in a bowl. I told this to Rory but she thought I was criticising him. 'You made your choices,' she said. And I have.

I used to think that Rory would be my guide dog when I went over the hill, would lead me into the new generation. Now I see that she was hanging around waiting for me to give her the vital information she needed to grow up. We have nothing to do with each other except love and guilt. The terms of reference change with the times and experience is wear-dated. She thinks I turned to packet foods and tabloid papers because I lost interest in life. In fact it is my interest in life that impels me to labour-saving food and literature – that and an aversion to eating anything that still looks like an animal, although I am too old now for the full routine of nuts and pulses. I talked to an Indian on the bus one day (you have to pick your company with care if you intend to say anything you mean) and told him how I could no longer bear to pick up a fish or a chicken and take it home and eat it, because I suddenly knew they were my brothers, but now I worried that such thinking might in due course lead to a meatless world in which the pleasant cow would become extinct. 'But the vast, intensified brotherhood of cows is ruining the ozone layer with its communal breaking of methane wind,' the Indian gentleman enlightened me. I found this exchange deeply satisfactory. How fitting for the Almighty to knock us all off with a massive cow fart.

What appeals to me now is the language of the tabloid. People do not fornicate or have carnal knowledge. They have sex romps. They frolic. They do not exceed the permitted number of alcohol units. They guzzle. 'He Guzzled Bubbly while he Peddled Death,' ran the banner headline above the story of a drugs dealer.

It is not, after all, a chapter of adult corruption but a nursery story of miracle babies and naughty children looking for pleasure or treasure, excitement or escape, and reigning over all is the breast goddess – the giver of forgiveness, of guzzling and joy.

Have we all been let down by our mothers who failed to frolic while we guzzled? Was little Marigold lucky, in spite of the bruises and her cold sleep, to have, for a little while, a mother young enough to romp? If only we had the right to choose.

I have a secret. When you get to my age, your fingers go numb and they lose their grip and then you can choose anything you fancy.

There is a photograph in my secret box of a man and a woman. They are not my parents because I was not born then, but I have chosen them. They do not smile. They watch the camera as if it was a test. The girl clasps her flowers like a doll. She has a dress with square buttons and a hat which claps its brim over her alarmed eyes. The man has a suit but he does not wear it, he is worn by it. Such pure people. When this is over, will they be allowed to take off their good clothes and play again?

After the wedding my mother told me they ate rashers and eggs in a hotel and drank champagne and then went to Blackpool on the boat.

In my mind's eye that is where I see them, leaning on the rail looking into the water that floated them away from the world of rules and responsibilities. They might have played

'I spy' or talked about the enormous meal they would eat when they got to their hotel – chicken and salad and soufflé and wine – for they were thin and were probably always hungry. Now and again the boy might have looked at the square buttons on the pale blue dress and thought: she's underneath there and she's my woman now. It is certain that they did not think about me for I did not exist then, just as they do not exist now, and did not exist after I was born and made them grow up. It is almost certain that they did not think about orgasms although they might have kissed and kissed until they were in an ecstasy of deprivation. They might have thought that ecstasy was just a tiny little moment away – a romp, a frolic, away – like the jam at the bottom of the pudding dish when you had eaten most of your rice.

Most likely they just thought that they had all the time in the world now; that they never, ever had to please anyone for the rest of their lives but themselves and one another, which were one and the same; that for tonight they might just hold each other close on the narrow bunk and rock to slumber on the waves and tomorrow, in private, in another country, start off their lives.

MARY O'DONNELL

Scavengers

J ack's house overlooks the seafront. On fogged winter
evenings when rehearsals are in full swing, mother
sometimes asks you to join her there, when you've done
your homework. They are assembled casually, principals and
perhaps a few of the chorus, the artistic soul of Clonfoy, once
more rallying to the call of art while the sea spitefully lashes
the harbour.

Nominally, it's a rehearsal. You know that by the time the
quartet from *The White Horse Inn*, or the chorus from *The Maid of
the Mountains* is sung, the serious business of the evening is over.
In a sense. Jack, who usually has a cameo role of some sort,
busies himself making tea, resplendent in a plum-coloured
satin smoking-jacket, while the ladies slice Swiss rolls and
sandwich-cakes.

You always go. Dorian is there. He pays scant attention to
you but at least you can pass a few hours within the aura of The
Presence. Jack's piano stands near the balcony windows and

41

Dorian flexes his fingers importantly, while the leads cluster close, eyeing the score intently.

'That was a bit sharp – take the last four bars again,' Dorian might say, to Cassie usually. Her voice is high and forced, the shrill discordance needling its way to the eardrums. Dorian winces slightly as she zooms off-key again, or slurs indulgently down from high soh to doh. What commences with patience on his part, deteriorates gradually to a sizzling restraint, as Cassie continues to strike sharp from time to time.

'Can't break her from that habit,' he says between his teeth to mother. 'No ear, you see. She can't hear it in her head.' You are dazzled. Even then, mother is half in love with him. He looks slightly ferocious, his fine dark hair hanging limply over a perspiring forehead.

'He's a true artist,' she claims by way of explanation, when Dorian becomes irritable with the chorus.

'He suffers for it,' she adds, shaking her head dolefully.

'Mm,' you reply acquiescently, determined to sound neutral.

'Why does he behave so stupidly when he's drunk then?' you ask disapprovingly in the next breath, unconsciously ferreting your way into a wound and rubbing salt into it. You've heard stories about Dorian's demented binges. Saw him carried on a stretcher off the lifeboat, trembling dreadfully. After he'd gone out in someone's skiff and run it into The Ridge. You remember the smell. The stench of alcohol and vomit. And father.

Mother pauses, takes a sharp breath to steel herself against the ignorance of extreme youth. 'He can't help it, Laura,' – she is nothing if not sympathetic – 'he's driven to it. Things get to him.'

You withdraw, wary of her insights.

One evening in early spring, she asks you to accompany her to Jack's, the fourth time in two weeks. You go anyway, enjoy watching the singers, listening to the tender humming and aahing as vocal chords are warmed up, primed amidst numerous arpeggios, the prelude to any musical rendering. You, of course, will never, ever, achieve their level of ease and gregariousness. Their music enthrals, despite Cassie of the dreaded F sharp. Count Danilo places his hands on Olga's waist and whirls her to his chest. You sit riveted. How can they *do* that without getting embarrassed, you ponder again. Mother sits on the piano-stool with Dorian. They play a duet. There is something rather sober-looking about them, compared to the others who by this stage have uncorked bottles of dark wine: love is as sombre as it is riotous, you discover. The music is like a twisting or stirring in your body, and perhaps somewhere else that doesn't have a name. It hurts, makes you sense happiness. You know that you will cry into the bedroom curtains when you get home, try to stifle this strange, churning sensation.

Then he asks her to sing, and you sense that she is pleased. 'Come on Toni,' he coaxes, 'try "I'm a Stranger in Paradise".' Before she can protest the first chords fill the room. The others gradually stop talking. Mother stands behind Dorian, gazes out the window as she sings, her eyes looking along the damp, narrow road that skirts the harbour, beyond the sulphurous yellow glow from the street lights. Everybody listens. She sways to the rhythm of the song. Their faces gradually cloud to seriousness. Then at the end, they clap and yahoo, and her eyes are bright, her smile nervous.

It is your last year, the final lap of an insufferable ordeal at the hands of fact-saturating bores. But on your treks to and from school, there is the possibility of meeting Dorian in his frosted blue Scirocco. He always sees you, waves casually or winks. You are convinced that he finds you attractive, ever since the evening at Jack's place when he remarked to someone that you had 'a nice little figure'. You are hungry for praise. Even these meagre crumbs satisfy. You learn what it is to scavenge, to gnaw on pickings, nibble on bones. Without any doubt, you know that mother has beaten you to it. The main kill. Without even trying. Dorian is hers, for no other reason except alignment of age, experience and attitude. She simply is.

So you bask in reflected light, something generated by others, pale as a winter sun by the time it reaches you. Sense conspiracies, yearn to be part of them. By comparison, school friendships are a web of crude emotions, as clumsy as large rusted nails driven crookedly into a frame, splintering the wood. The day is a prohibitive sequence of bells and instructions, well-meant advice and reprimands.

'If your poor father could see you now . . .'

'It still affects her, you know . . .'

'The mother exercises no control . . .'

Words, words, filter through to your consciousness. They offend. Yet your dreams stay intact. Other words like 'bohemian', 'cosmopolitan' and 'experienced' rise from the bed of your mind, move like a slow tide around your waking thoughts, dispel the fear of stumbling feet and the coarse tongue that went with it. They kept you both silent. After the funeral, you cried with relief. A sweet, flushing relief.

You arrive home one day to find your mother and Dorian in the sitting-room. They have been laughing. You hear their voices as you open the back door, follow the sound, surprised to have visitors. Normally she rests or applies face-packs and eye-balms. 'Ah, you're here, Laura!' – a little over-enthusiastic. They sit smiling at you, cups empty, crumbs on the coffee-table. You brace yourself. She gets straight to the point.

'Laura . . .' Hesitantly, fingers joined for a moment, as if unsure of what to say. Much like the way she joins her fingers before she sings. Preparing. Focusing her thoughts on something important.

'Dorian and I are thinking of taking a holiday soon. Maybe around Hallowe'en, we thought.'

We thought. Dorian and I. Mother you're even sillier than I thought, and you know how he drinks, you know, you know.

'Yeah?' you grunt by way of a reply, attempting the road of neutrality, trying to strike an appropriate pose, to arrange your face in an expression of mild surprise and a less-than-tepid interest.

'Good idea!' you add then, more jauntily.

'Where d'you think you'll go?' you continue, feigning concessionary interest, determined to control yourself, to quiet the resentment that steams your mind with its heat.

'Well, we thought maybe London . . .'

Great. Just great. A furtive weekend in the metropolis. You force your face into a congratulatory, approving smile.

'Sounds great to me anyway,' and you shrug your shoulders.

Their relief is instant. It flows osmotically through the room from their bodies. You stroll out again, head for the piano in the other room. You cannot muster the energy to attempt the 'Polonaise', the 'Marche Militaire', or 'Zug der Zwerge'. You tinkle apathetically for some time, fingers on automatic control, while your mind rages within its confines. You cannot cry. Not yet, not yet. Crying belongs to the night, in the oceanic quiet of dark, the secret peace, when the beast moves out, far out across the rocks, into the heaving breast of the sea, to thresh in its lonely turmoil.

You have lost the morsels of Dorian's attention that used to fall down your open gullet. His glances. A chance touch against your arm. Things mother seems not to notice, or if she does, not to care about. That afternoon, he stays to tea, and afterwards they drive to Jack's, for one final rehearsal of *The Gondoliers*. A family again. Whole and complete. Wheee! They sing even as they leave – 'Dance a Cachuca, Fandango, Bolero'. Your face feels unbearably heavy as you hear their jokes and remarks. How childish they are.

You can't prevent yourself thinking about them, about what they are going to do in London. It does not dawn on you that they have probably done it already. You have a highly developed sense of protocol, and London, or somewhere labelled 'away', is the appropriate location for the consummation of such matters. You retire early, shored-up. A grotesque untouchable whose needs are of such abnormal proportions that none must ever guess at the quivering beast that lies seconds behind your smooth face.

All through the musical 'season' you simmer, smart inwardly each time you examine her bright face, focused on Dorian's equally radiant one. The house is filled with music. You cannot wake in the mornings without hearing mother's voice as she practises scales after the ritual drink of hot honey and lemon. To soothe the vocal chords. You tire of the 'Cachuca, Fandango, Bolero', and 'The Duke of Plaza-Toro', the vigorous renderings of which now seem incessant and a necessary component of life at home.

There is no escape. You pass the concert-hall one evening just as the chorus is belting out the finale. The audience is clapping in time to the music. This makes it for the singers, if not for Dorian, who never admits to being pleased about any show, by way of implying how impossibly high his standards are. In an instant, you see what it all means. Camaraderie and rivalry. What it means to recognise that Cassie is singing sharp once again. What it means to dance in a dress with a velvet bodice that pinches your waist. What it is to hear applause because the audience likes your music, likes what you love, what is inextricably part of you because it forces you to feel things. We push at the horizon, all of us. At any minute, we could be being born, might break the skin that separates us from ourselves, but it is a hungry struggle, a dark, vital, passion-ridden business that begs to be satisfied. So much of it is hunger.

The next morning you expect mother to be buoyant. Instead, she sits rather despondently at breakfast, as you rush around, late as usual. Her dressing-gown hangs half-open, and for the first time since father's death she is smoking.

'Cigarettes?' you half-squeak.

She glances up. You might be a crustacean that has wandered in from the shore during the night.

'Ah . . .' she sighs, runs her hand back through her hair. Traces of Leichner make-up have yellowed the roots at the front.

'I just felt like one, and the show's over anyway.'

'But your voice, mother . . .' you begin hastily.

She interrupts swiftly, will not suffer fools at this early hour. 'Won't do me any harm – this once,' and she smiles by way of silencing you. A patronising smile, reserved only for the young or the infirm. You pull the door sharply. Quite clearly, she thinks you know nothing. Understand nothing. You long for revenge of some sort, sit nettled all day, absorbed in the plot of *Retribution*, a drama in three parts which will take place at some indeterminate juncture of your future.

Nevertheless, when she invites you to accompany her to Jack's for one last round of songs before the society breaks up for a few months, you cannot resist. Their world still beckons, subtly and forcefully, seduces like a wholesome meal. Oddly enough, Dorian is absent. Jack mumbles something to mother, who looks disconcerted. You scrutinise her face. It betrays little, but when she speaks, you notice that her voice has lost its smoothness, presents a rasping quality which hitherto had not been there. She's been smoking all day. Someone plays the piano, leads into a set of numbers from past shows – *Showboat*, *Porgy and Bess*, *Kismet*. Soon the room is warm, throbs with the sound of sopranos, altos, baritones, Jeanette MacDonalds and Count John McCormacks. They sway together, look pleased and serious, wrapped in their own virtuosity.

Just as they prepare to launch into the second verse of 'Good-bye' where bold Leopold marches off for the sake of the fatherland, a car skids wildly to a halt somewhere beyond the house. To my surprise, everyone grows silent. Mother looks anxious. She is flushed. Twists her fingers uneasily, runs her rings up and over the knuckles. The fellow at the piano attempts to stoke things up again, but the moment has passed. The doorbell rings. 'Who the hell can that be?' Jack, muttering, glances quickly at her. There's a lot of noise in the hall then, the sound of heavy footsteps, the door slamming loudly. Above it all, Dorian's voice, garrulous.

He stumbles in. Suddenly the men are around him, saying things like 'You're all right, you're all right,' and 'Take it easy now.' But he doesn't. You shrink at the tirade, words vile and insulting. You don't understand everything. His mouth is twisted and ugly, flaps uselessly, like a torn pocket. Then he turns on mother. Moves towards her. She stands up.

'Toni,' he begins, leaning against her, talking into her face. You can smell his breath from where you sit. Reel with a nauseous sense of nightmare. Nightmare. Night-mare. *Mare*: sea. Neuter noun. Third declension. That steely darkness whence the beast comes at dawn, returns at night. How often he did that. Came and went. Came and went, like a violent tide, battering you both into submission. Over and over.

His eyes, red-rimmed and watery, peer into her face. Saliva trembles on his lower lip. You want to close your eyes.

'Not now, Dorian,' she says gently, trying to push him from her. Her gentleness is beyond you.

'Not now,' he repeats thickly, while the others whisper, or try to pretend that nothing untoward is occurring.

'Not now?' he repeats, his voice rising in a drunken question. He pauses, calling on the remnants of his consciousness, sways slightly. 'Well *when*?' he roars, his fingers gripping the top of her arm. Sweat rolls on your back and your eyes prickle with the threat of tears.

Suddenly her expression is one of helplessness. He launches into an incoherent stream of language which strikes your ears like grapeshot. He shouts, makes ugly sounds with ugly words. You remember the words 'merry' and 'widow', his mocking tone, his fist coming down on the piano keyboard as he chants a few bars of the waltz. Jack tries to intervene with pleas of 'That's enough now, that's enough,' and someone else keeps repeating 'You're all right, you're all right,' while he tears at her flesh, strips her of music, of love, spits all in her face. He actually spits at her. Somebody starts to pat your shoulder then. You roar back that it isn't all right, your face crumpling in on itself as the sobbing begins. As something hateful and familiar begins to circle your brain, treading, treading, a tormented hunger, pacing, pacing, locked within itself, focused on the sight of father's face, ridiculously peaceful after the accident.

Yet this time, you cry for her. All the way home, she drives with her face set rigidly, while you sniffle in the passenger seat. You have not anticipated such a dénouement, such humiliation, have misinterpreted the signs and the skies. It is so undignified. So devoid of all that you cherish. There is baseness everywhere. For the first time in your life, you pity your mother, want so to recreate the world that she might be spared Dorian, his demonic binges. That she, that you both, might know what is real, might reject the wild spawn of a charlatan muse.

As you get out of the car, you blow your nose. She locks up, walks ahead to the front door. Stops then, and turns to you, her eyes large and tired. A foghorn blows, long and sonorous, and grey mist smothers the windows and roofs of every house. How ghostly she is then. You shut the door on the town, in an effort to seal off the talk which, inevitably, will break like a flood-tide the next day, frothy with inaccuracies and frequent re-telling. Stuff that will be sniffed at, picked over behind safe walls, till the bones are well-exposed.

BERNARD MacLAVERTY

In Bed

The buzzer sounded long and hard – a rasp which startled her even though she knew to expect it – maybe *because* she knew to expect it. She splayed her book on the carpet so as not to lose her place and went across the hall to her daughter's bedroom – moving quickly because the long buzz created a sense of urgency. The girl was crouched on the bed, her face turned towards the door in panic.

'Mum, another one,' she said and pointed to her hand pressed down hard on the pillow.

'Take it easy. Relax.' Her mother hurried out of the bedroom and came back with an empty pint glass from the kitchen.

'How can I relax with a thing like that in bed? It might breed, might be laying eggs.'

'Wait.'

'Dad uses a bar of soap. Don't let it get away.' The girl's face was anxious and much whiter than usual. She was wearing pyjama bottoms and a football shirt of red and white hoops.

'I hate them – I hate them.' Her voice was shaking. Her mother approached the pillow with the pint glass inverted.

'Easy now – lift your hand.'

The girl plucked her hand away. The black speck vanished – it was there, then, suddenly, it wasn't – before the glass could be slammed down. The girl screamed.

'It's jumped.'

'Blast.'

The girl held her hair back from her face, peering down at the surface of the sheet.

'It's gone – it's got away.'

'Aw no . . .'

'Oh I hate them, I really hate them.' The girl's voice was on the edge of tears. She was shuddering. 'They make me feel so . . . dirty.' Her mother bent over and stared closely at the surface of the white sheet, pulling it towards her a little to flatten a wrinkle.

'Don't move,' she whispered. The girl gave a little gasp.

'Where? Where is it?'

Her mother raised the glass and quickly pressed it down onto the sheet.

'Gotcha.'

The girl bent over and looked inside. She pulled up her lip in distaste when she saw the black speck.

'Eucchh.' It jumped again and she squealed even though it was inside the glass. 'I'm never going to let that cat in here again. I hate it.'

'Take over,' said her mother. 'Press it down tight. Don't let it out.'

She went out of the bedroom and her daughter heard her filling a basin with water. She pressed the glass down until her arm ached. The rim of the glass dug into the sheet and made the centre swell like a pin-cushion. The flea disappeared.

'Oh no. Mum!' She put her face down close. The black speck reappeared. Her mother came back, forced to take short steps with the weight in the plastic basin. Some of the water slopped over the sides and formed droplets on the carpet.

'Here,' she said. 'Let me at it.' She set the basin on the floor and looked around. She took a Get Well card from the mantelpiece and turned it over to the plain white side. Her daughter let go of the glass and the mother began to slide the card beneath it while still pressing down.

'Don't let it get away,' said the girl. She was holding her hair back with a hand on either side of her face. The black speck was flinging itself into the roof of the pint glass.

'Easy does it.' Her mother completed sliding the card all the way across. She picked the whole lot up and showed it to the girl. The trapped speck did not move.

'They're so thin,' said the daughter. 'One-dimensional.'

'Two-dimensional – that's so's they can move through the animal's fur.' Her mother squatted down beside the basin and held the glass over the water. 'I feel like a priestess or a magician or something. A new rite. Releasing the flea. Dah-dah.' She lowered the card partially into the water then withdrew it, leaving the flea floating. They both peered closely at it.

'Look at the legs – the length of them,' said the girl, leaning over the side of her bed. Her mother nodded.

'That's why they can jump over the Eiffel Tower.'

The flea was in a panic, cycling round the surface of the water, travelling backwards. The girl flopped back on her pillows, panting.

'Oh God,' she said.

'What?'

'That's really exhausted me.'

'Rest for a while.' The girl nodded. She was very white now.

'You've ruined my card,' she said. 'It looks all weepy.' The water had made the ink run. Her mother patted it dry against the carpet.

'It's an old one,' she said.

'I like to keep them all. Let me see it.' Her mother turned over the face of the card and handed it to her. It was a picture of a person in bed covered from head to foot in bandages. 'Oh, that's really ancient – two years ago, at least. From Johnny.' All the volume had drained out of her voice.

Her mother was bent over still staring at the flea.

'It's not floating,' she said. 'Surface tension. It's in a kind of dimple on the surface.' She looked up at her daughter but the girl didn't move. She just lay there with the card in her hand and her eyes closed. She could hear her breathing through her nose.

With her finger she sank the flea to the bottom of the basin and got up and tip-toed out.

About an hour later the buzzer rasped again and the mother went in.

'Could I have my tea now?'

'Anything to eat?'

'One bit of toast – no marmalade.'

When the supper was made she carried in the tray and set it on the chest of drawers. She pulled her daughter up into a sitting position, and propped her large sitting-up pillow behind her, then put the tray across her knees.

'Do you want me to stay?'

The girl shrugged. 'Whatever you like.' The wind rattled the windows and rain scudded against the panes. Her mother sat down on a bedside chair.

'It's a terrible night.'

The girl nodded and sipped her tea. The draught made her mobile rotate. A year ago, when she'd rallied slightly, she'd lain on her side in the darkened room and, with a little help from her father, had made a papier-mâché model of the sun. She was pleased with it. Then she made the earth and moon in the months that followed. When they were all finished she said, 'And on the seventh month she rested.' Now the heavenly bodies hung from the ceiling on threads above her bed. 'Give me something to stare at,' she'd said. 'Like a baby in her pram.' The earth was realistic, with blue oceans and brown-coloured land, but the sun and moon had faces. The yellow sun had spikes radiating from it and half the grey moon's face was covered in black shadow.

'How's our friend getting along?' said her mother. She looked towards the basin still on the floor.

'How does anything travel like that? It just hurls itself anywhere. Doesn't know if it's going to land in the fire – or my tea or anywhere.'

'A leap in the dark,' said her mother and smiled.

'What a life.' She bit at the edge of her piece of toast. 'Well, it's over now.'

'So . . .' Her mother leaned back in the chair and joined her hands behind her head. From the quiet tone of voice the girl knew immediately what was going to be said.

'This has been a better . . . It's been a less bad month.'

'I don't want to talk about it.'

The girl chewed her toast – then leaned forward to take a sip of the tea. She always drank it hot with very little milk in it.

'Compared to this time last year,' said the mother.

The girl's voice was on the edge of tears so the mother stopped talking. Her daughter rubbed her eyes, then stared straight in front of her, still chewing.

'Where's Dad?'

'He took your wee sister to the pictures. Just to get out.'

'What's the film?'

'Something in the Odeon. With Matt Dillon in it.'

'He's amazing.'

The sun swung almost imperceptibly from side to side. The earth turned slowly to face the moon.

'Any time we got a flea at home,' said her mother, 'it was blamed on the picture house. I used to come up in lumps and Mum'd say, "When were you last at the pictures?" There was never any possibility that you could've picked it up in church.'

'Or school.' She lifted her tray off her knees and offered it to her mother. 'I'm too tired. I'll have to lie down.' She toppled her sitting-up cushion onto the floor and keeled over flat on the bed. Her mother set the tray on the dressing-table and sat down on the chair again. She said,

'Take it easy.'

After a moment the girl leaned over and looked at the basin on the floor.

'Where is it?'

'It's still there. Don't panic.'

'Give me the backscratcher.'

Her mother handed it to her. It was a stick with a small fake hand at the end of it, the fingers curled up. The girl dipped it into the water and tried to squash the flea between the plastic knuckles and the bottom of the basin.

'Love . . .' Again the quiet tone.

'Talking about it doesn't change anything.'

'It gives a purpose. Goals. Something to aim at.'

The girl had turned the plastic hand round and was now trying to cradle the flea in its palm. Every time she brought it to the surface the flea slipped sideways off into the water.

'What's the point?' she said.

'You're sick. You're twenty-one years of age. You've improved. Someday you'll be better. We have to prepare for that. Aim at it.'

'Huh.' She rolled her eyes away from her mother and looked up at the papier-mâché globes above her. 'Improved.' Her eyes filled with tears. Then she whipped the backscratcher down onto the surface of the water with a slap, splashing it over the carpet. She buried her face in her arm. She was half shouting words, half crying them – this is what talking about it does, she was trying to say. Her mother went to sit on the bed beside her and put an arm around her shoulder. The girl was shuddering and shouting into her hair and the crook of her arm and the tumbled sheets. Her words were wet and distorted.

'I'm not, I'm not,' said her mother. 'Not for one minute am I blaming you. All I'm saying is that this time last year – no, two years ago – you couldn't get to the bathroom on your own . . .' The mother held tightly onto her daughter's shoulder. It was sharp with thinness under the material of the football shirt. Eventually the girl stopped crying. Her mother went to the bathroom and damped a face-cloth with hot water and brought it to her.

'Crying doesn't help,' said the girl. 'Nothing helps.' The cloth steamed as it was opened. Her mother massaged her daughter's face. 'What time will Dad be back?'

'Ten? Half ten?'

The girl leaned out of bed, picked up the backscratcher again and began to stir the basin with it.

'Maybe don't tell him I was crying.'

'Okay.'

She withdrew the plastic hand and this time the flea was stuck to the back of it. She brought it up close to her face to inspect it, curling up her lip as she did so. Suddenly it jumped.

'It's alive,' she screamed.

'I don't believe it. It can't be.'

'It is.'

'God Almighty.'

Both women squealed and laughed with the shock it had given them.

'The flea jumped over the moon,' said the girl and continued to laugh. She lay back on her pillows, her shoulders shaking, her hand over her mouth. Her mother smiled and straightened out the coverlet. She bent over, her eyes only inches above it, staring.

'Right,' she said, '– let's take it from the very beginning.' Her mother searched every visible inch of the coverlet but could see nothing. 'Don't worry – we'll find it before it finds you. It's only a matter of time.' She reached out and with a licked finger touched every speck.

In Bed

'No.'
Every black particle.
'No.'
Any crumb.
'Definitely not.'
The girl listened to her mother's voice with closed eyes.

MARY LELAND

The Little Galloway Girls

'Picture!' Sr Perpetua used to say. Elizabeth unconsciously echoed her as she opened the newspaper and startled her sisters with her exclamation.

'Picture!'

They gathered at the round table at which the pages were spread, and three pairs of eyes stared at the photograph and its caption: 'Lady Elizabeth Holderness presents the Gascoyne Trophy for the best Jersey bull at the Spring Show in Dublin yesterday. Accepting the prize is breeder Jeremiah Long, Longfield, Co. Down, with his bull Sherman.'

'There's no Ross!' wailed Frances, and the others smiled at her mock indignation. She was the one who was proudest of her second name – 'I'm Frances Ross Galloway, if you please,' her five-year-old self had announced on her arrival at the convent, an announcement that had gone into the annals of the school's reprobates. Up to then only the Reverend Superior had known that the two other girls were Elizabeth Holderness

Galloway and Louise Gascoyne Galloway, but Frances, never again in her life to be called Fanny, had alerted the staff to the Ascendancy ring of their names.

'But the nuns all have double-barrelled names,' protested Louise when she realised how the knowledge was to be used against them. 'There's Sr Margaret of the Sacred Heart, and Mother Mary Theresa, and Sr Martin de Porres – why are they getting at us?'

Elizabeth, the eldest at eight, had been unable to explain it. It was one more manifestation of the effects of the earthquake in their lives. All she had been able to do in their suddenly extraordinary circumstances was retreat totally from confrontation so as to remain the single sister not incapacitated by punishment restrictions.

This may have been partly as a result of her experience of life with their father whom, as she told them when necessary, she had known longer than they had. Her earliest emotional memory was of pity for her mother, whose bursts of resistance she witnessed, and whose despairing acquiescence she came to despise.

Contempt is a sophisticated emotion, and Elizabeth did not handle it very well. It was what distinguished her immediately among her school-fellows, and it encouraged the conclusion of the Reverend Mother that she was a devious, intractable child.

Even the Reverend Mother had to admit that there was something winning about Louise. She had a willingness to be good, to be unremarkable at least, which the nuns thought would allow her to be rescued. As for Frances – the child was young, of course, but could not be allowed to become the baby of the convent because of the strong will and obdurate, self-confident temperament immediately displayed.

Reverend Mother would be the first to admit – indeed she was – that taking three young sisters into the school all at the same time presented problems, and that the potential for trouble was emphasised by the background of the little Galloway girls. Beginning with that unfortunate, impetuous marriage – perhaps that was where Frances got her stubbornness? – and the father's life abroad while his wife reared the children in Kilkenny, well, who could wonder if, the difference in religion apart, the couple came to grief? And once that had happened, and the mother had left, how could any conscientious religious teaching community refuse the father's plea to house and educate his children?

'You can see my position, Mother Benignus,' he explained while the deal was negotiated.

'Those girls have been left to run wild. Plenty of money, I sent all I could, and there was plenty. But she never understood the rearing of children. When I was at home I tried to insist on a pattern that would remain when I had to go off again, but of course she ignored that as soon as my back was turned. And of course I asked the priest to keep an eye on the girls going to Mass and all that sort of thing, but she resented his calls and do you know, really, I think she began to resent every Catholic she knew in the end?'

Mother Benignus was shocked, of course, but she was a woman of the world if any Mother Superior was, and she knew the way things could turn out. Nor was she without heart – and besides, although she would never, ever admit it even to herself – it was all so interesting.

'So very young, wasn't she, Mrs Galloway? And yourself

too, of course, Mr Galloway. You know, it may even turn out
to be all for the best, God moves in most mysterious ways.'

'Oh, there were plenty to tell us we were doing the wrong
thing. And I hardly knew her – hardly knew her. All we needed
was to think the world against us, and we did, so there was
nothing for us to do but marry and be damned to them all.
With respects to you, Reverend Mother.'

'Ah, Mr Galloway. It's not the first story of that kind that
I've heard. It is always hard for our young men working in
England, so many of them are fooled by that gentle English
charm. So sweet, of course. Anyone could understand.'

'Well.' He was curt. He knew the nun understood the
economics of Catholicism, that he would be paying the bill
for his daughters and that it was her business to placate him,
to condole.

'Anyway. You know what I want, now. No letters from
her. No visits. That's the only way. They have to be weaned.
Weaned from her.'

The word with its echoes of milky maternity mocked him
by its unconscious repetition.

'Separated. She isn't going to fight the case in the court so
we will have a legal separation within the next six months.
After that she'll have no call even to try to get here, so the
important thing until then will be to keep them apart. They're
still young, you know. She has influence.'

Only over her daughters, that was. And only in so
far as a timid character, however kind, can have until
a stronger one opposes it. Both Sr Benignus and Mr
Galloway knew that pretty Mrs Galloway had no influence
that mattered – no money, no family, no friends who could
be called on in Ireland. The children were to be rescued

from her as from the burning, saved from Anglicism as from hell.

'Picture that!' was Sr Perpetua's response to small Fanny's nomination of herself as a person of consequence, but there was no satire in the remark, no desire to deflate unsuitable pretension. Frances Ross Galloway recognised in the nun some familiarity with the importance of nomenclature, some willingness to accept that a child might have status.

'That's just because Daddy's grandmother was a Ross,' Elizabeth pronounced when Louise tried to wonder why Frances kept on about it.

'It was Mammy kept on giving her the full name, I think she thought Daddy would like it. Not like us.'

No, the two eldest had been named to reflect the English lines; when they were older the girls were to ponder this – after all the marriage had been made in haste. Why call up the opposition in naming the offspring?

Again it was Elizabeth who came close to an answer then:

'He just had an eye out for the main chance. He must have thought Mammy was well-connected. The names do sound rather grand. Perhaps she told him lies.'

'Perhaps she told him the truth, and he didn't believe her.' Louise by then had no memory of her mother, and had created a comfortingly beautiful, truthful, misunderstood being to take her place.

These were the mysteries of their lives. Elizabeth was the one to pronounce on them, for she was the eldest, and she was the one who had had the adventure.

Although not comfortable, the convent was clean and warm. Set on a slight eminence halfway along the street of a village, it had not been remote, but remained sternly untouched by the life which wavered around the gates. The school also took in day-girls from the immediate area, but most of its pupils were boarders, children of strong farmers and the less ambitious professionals. The nuns were of the same stock as the pupils, sturdy, unimaginative, devout.

The little Galloway girls were immediately recognised as not the same.

'Protestant,' whispered one of the prefects gathered in council around the Head Girl. 'A mixed marriage!' the others breathed back, their eyes brighter for this vision of a sin so mortal as to be beyond their wildest imaginings. The Head Girl resisted the romance; the girls were baptised Catholics, it was just that their mother had been English. And – as she dropped her voice the others crouched closer to hear the wonderful words – 'And – the mother ran away! Left her husband!'

Who had told them this? Not the people who told Elizabeth, for no one told Elizabeth. There had been a furious bustle in the cottage near Kilkenny town, her mother preparing for the return of their father just before Christmas. Rubbish was burned, bags and newspapers and magazines and even old clothes and shoes. Louise and Fanny were given the job of touring the neighbourhood, as far as their small feet would carry them, with a box filled with seven kittens, the rival litters of two cats, in order to find homes for them.

Two shopkeepers had taken an animal each; the little Galloway girls were liked in the town, and when people talked of them it seemed as if their mother was included in the appellation. The children trudged to the mill, where the cashier took one out of pity for them, asking her brother to drown it when she got it home. Some of the men gathered around them, their hands floury cradles for the kittens, assessing them with kind jokes. Three more were taken. The girls knew they would be safe there, would grow fat on rats and milk. But they were left with one. Fanny began to cry, she was so tired and so weighted with this final responsibility. Louise declared that she didn't care, she was too hungry and her feet were sore and she was going home with the kitten, no matter what their father might say.

In the cold dusk they tried to run, but the kitten kept slipping from their arms as they took turns in carrying it, and finally Louise dropped it altogether so that it scampered away into the weeds by the river-bank and what with tears and the dim light and the damp on the grasses they could neither find it nor decide where to look. Fanny said and said ever afterwards that she could hear it crying, but Louise insisted that it was gone and that it would find somewhere safe for itself until the morning and that Mammy would murder them if they didn't get home, it must be very late.

There were lights on in all the rooms so that the cottage looked larger than it ever seemed to the children, who lived most of the time in the kitchen and shared only one of the bedrooms. Elizabeth was carrying a box of bottles out to the shed, and Mrs Galloway, sitting at the kitchen table writing out a list, only glanced at the girls and told them there was a pan of fried potatoes in the range for their supper. She never asked why Fanny was crying, and she never asked them about the kittens. And they never told her.

The floor of the kitchen was flagged with smooth stones on which pretty rugs were thrown. The furniture was big, old and battered, but there was a softness to it appreciated by both people and cats, and here and there on the painted walls hung pictures brought back by Mr Galloway from London, and in the corners huge pottery jars, made in the surprising sheds of Englishmen living in the county, were full of dried rushes the children gathered, and bunches of preserved flowers Mr Galloway brought from Paris. While the two younger girls were out, the range had been blacked and the dresser dusted, the floors swept throughout the long cold passage linking the rooms. Holly from the tree in the garden was laid along the windowsills and over the mantel-shelf, and a few early Christmas cards gaily straddled a string across the back door.

Elizabeth bent and lifted over the rubble piled on the floor, and the cards shifted in the light chill breeze that floated through every time she took another bundle out to the shed. Mrs Galloway finished writing; she owed a total of £117 and 14 shillings to the shop-keepers of the town, and wondered how it had happened, what he would say. Getting up, she twisted the piece of paper and thrust it into the fire, adding to the sudden blaze the brown envelope for the parish dues, the accumulated and by now threatening notes from the school, the postcard in a masculine hand with a date and a place and a time written on it and nothing else.

Now she should wash the girls' hair and dry off their good clothes before the fire so they would be presentable when he came the next day. She looked at them, Elizabeth sitting at her supper where Loulou and Fanny had finished. Three pairs of brown eyes looked solemnly back at her, three white faces spoke of exhaustion and anxiety.

They looked foreign to her, as alien as everything in this

town had been since her husband selected the picturesque cottage as the home for them until he could live in Ireland permanently and find a larger place. Would that day ever come? She didn't ask whether she wanted it to; life had an inevitability for her, its phases dictated by the will of other people. But these three little people were her own, as it struck her now.

'You're great girls. But we're all too tired now to do any more. I'm sure everything will be all right. Let's go to bed. And let's have a treat: you can all jump in with me, just for tonight. We'll keep each other warm.'

Elizabeth remembered that as a treat, all tucked up together in the big brass bed, bigger and brassier as she remembered, but indeed it had been big enough for the four slender bodies. Louise did not remember it at all but thought she did, lace-hung and with a canopy. Frances dreamed all through her life afterwards, when her dreams were happy, that she was asleep in someone's arms, but she could never tell whose arms they were.

Sr Perpetua put her arms around her, once. The nun had only been a postulant then, of course. Still called Sr Margaret Rose. Her mother, Mother Benignus decided, must have been mad out of her mind over royalty, and she insisted that until her Profession the young aspirant would be called only Sr Margaret. But Sr Margaret had confided in Frances as she held the child on her lap. They sat in the huge, bright kitchen, every scoured pan and plate put away in the painted caverns of cupboards. She had found Frances at the Marian grotto, crying as she tried to reach one of the convent kittens which had trapped itself on the highest stones. The child wanted to rescue the little animal, but also she wanted to hold it, to feel it, to feel through it some trace of a familiar atmosphere, of something before the convent.

The postulant was an agile girl, the youngest child in a family of four older brothers. The kitten's wails and the little girl's gasping pleas spurred her to undignified action as she kilted her black skirt and jumped first and then climbed the bulging stone. To Frances' shocked eyes she was going away from the kitten, but Sr Margaret Rose knew a thing or two about frightened cats and climbed above it in order to reach down and grasp it firmly around the neck.

'Picture that!' Sr Margaret Rose laughed when she got to the ground again, handing the spitting bundle of fur to Frances. 'She scratched me. Picture!' She held out the thin seam across the palm of her hand, the translucent skin threaded with red berries. Frances began to sob again, the kitten had escaped her frenzied clutch, and the nun promised her it would find its way to the kitchens without their help. She had to go and wash her hand; would Frances come?

All the smells of all the dinners the girls would ever have in that school welcomed them to the chilly domesticity of the institution, but it was there none the less that Frances found a perch, and even when Sr Margaret Rose had become Sr Perpetua and a figure of some assumed authority the child sensed from her an aura of furtive comfort. Both Louise and Elizabeth shared that suspicion – that with Sr Perpetua there would be some slackening of the rule that the little Galloway girls were to be shown no special favour because of their youth, or their abandonment to the convent.

It was Sr Perpetua who obtained from her own sister-in-law the length of netted veil and the tiara of white satin roses for Frances, to soften the blunt wool ordered by Mother

Benignus and paid for by Mr Galloway for her First Holy Communion.

There were other feast-days; with the other girls the little Galloways were confirmed in their religion, attended the annual school concert for parents and dignitaries of the parish, sang at the Mass celebrating the transformation of Sr Margaret Rose into Sr Perpetua, and mourned easily with the rest of the school when an old nun died.

Now Sr Perpetua wore the harsh white headband and black veil of the other sisters. Her brown curls were hidden forever, and her hands were carried out of sight within the folded sleeves of the habit. Yet she was still the leaven in the hard bread of the children's existence, the adult to whom they referred for ease or comfort or explanation.

'She was a good nun!' Louise protested years later.

'It was easy to be good, if you were a nun at all,' retorted Elizabeth. 'But they had such a queer way of showing their goodness, and she wasn't any different, really. She kept the same rules, the same way of looking at things, as they did.'

'No.' Louise was able to insist. 'Perpetua was different. She was good because she was holy, really holy. And that made her kinder.'

'She was – *inspired*,' said Frances who was to remember all her life the yellow soap smell from Sr Perpetua's bodice. Choosing her word carefully, she repeated: 'Inspired. She was given the grace to see that the other nuns were right. *We were* different; we upset them. But she was happy in her life so she couldn't be upset, and so she could afford to think about us. I think that's inspiration.'

Elizabeth and Louise looked at her. She was saying the kind of thing that Louise liked to hear, but to Elizabeth her words

were a reminder of the way in which Frances could mull over
the experiences of her life and produce them as something
deeper, more important, different.

'None of those women were inspired. They didn't know
the meaning of the word – if they did they couldn't possibly
have lived as they did, in that convent, with those weak
forbidding priests telling them what to think, and all their
lives concentrating on learning their own rules and shoving
them into the children they were supposed to be minding.'

Frances smiled: 'Not minding us, Elizabeth. Educating
us.'

Louise was still anxious. 'But they entered because something urged them, they had an idea of a life of work and
prayer. And sacrifice. Didn't they?'

'Sacrifice?' Elizabeth was scornful. 'What sacrifice? What
were they giving up? What did they have to be renounced,
to be laid at the altar?'

'Opportunities?' offered Louise.

'They wouldn't know what to do with opportunities,' said
Elizabeth, who did.

They had been in the convent for two incredible weeks
when she first noticed, at a wicket gate leading into the town's
street, a dark-coated woman standing still in the doorway of a
shop opposite. Although it was February, and cold, the woman
wore no gloves, and her very long, very pale fingers clutched
a hand-bag which Elizabeth recognised, a glowing square of
red leather inlaid with tapestry panels of golden threads.

'Mammy!' she screamed, and her ecstatic cry sounded out so
loud that the woman withdrew immediately into the shadow
of the door where other people were going in and out and
someone briefly stopped to look around.

Elizabeth ran to the railings, to the wicket; she rattled it but it was locked. Hot desperate tears flooded her throat but when she looked across the road again the woman was outside the shop and laid a white finger against her lips, looking at Elizabeth as she did so. The child quietened at once and stood still.

Her mother walked carefully across the road. Her face was set, dead. A fringe of her black hair flopped from her headscarf, blues and reds and yellows that the girls had loved in a length of shimmering silk.

'Hide them!' She pushed a bag of brown paper through the iron spokes. 'I'll come again soon –' But the child interrupted her.

'Take us home, Mammy! Take us home. We'll be good, we'll go to school. We'll go to Mass; Fanny hasn't stopped asking when are we going home. Tell Daddy we'll be good –'

'Hush!' Her mother's word was fierce and sharp. 'I'll try to come again. You must stay where you are. My darling. My darlings. I'm sorry.' She turned away, and Elizabeth howled as she watched her mother becoming a woman in a dark coat walking away from her, leaving her behind.

This was what made Elizabeth furtive.

'Secretive,' Mother Benignus announced, at last, finding the true word to describe the escaped personality of the child who was never detected in actual wrong-doing.

Not like Frances, hauled in screams of tears from class because she would persist in saying *ay* instead of *ah*, *shall* instead of *will*, all the Anglicisations the nuns abhorred. To Frances these were like threads to a web, membership of the mesh of the world beyond the convent walls, beyond which she rarely went.

The brown bags brought by Elizabeth from a place she would not divulge were not threads, but claws. The buns inside them, stale but sticky, had a taste which hurt her heart. For a while, like Elizabeth, she had found a perch on the old stone wall of the convent's flower-garden from where she could see the green dust announcing the daily bus and for a while she thought she would wait, but it grew cold, and she did not know what it was she awaited, and one day there was something else to do. But she held on still to those things that made her different, so that when the other girls in her class, in her dormitory, reminded one another that they must not have too much to do with the Galloways they all understood that there was, indeed, some reason even if they could not tell what it was.

These years for the three girls were not all barren. There were school outings; there were games, a rough scramble with hurley-sticks after a small stitched ball with a vicious bite to the hand or the face; there were concerts. There were occasional friendlinesses from among the students, for they were not the only misfits and other, rescuing parents came and took them out to tea, or to the cinema.

There were visits from their father. On the first of these the girls were too frightened to ask him about their mother. All he represented to them was some earlier hint of guilt, a reason for hiding things, for hiding themselves. The sound of him was the sound of a storm in the night which blew their home away and banished their mother, the noise of loud hard words which made Mrs Craig, from the Rectory, apologise stiffly for interfering, but . . . With terrified eyes they saw her blush and turn back to the bright green gate between the holly trees, the berries no redder than her mortified face.

When the black car drew up so close to the gate that its door opened into the gap they entered it as though they were entering a tunnel of shame, and it was not until days later in the convent, when Louise discovered that she was to wear a nightdress in the bath, that humiliation broke in and grief and loneliness and bewilderment clattered and sprawled and beat at her in great wet clouts. Elizabeth too had wept but quietly, she would not let them see, but Frances had torn off the small shift in a rage and stepped into the bath threatening to bite anyone who tried to put it back on her. The scandal of that episode lingered for the rest of the school, but no one but the nuns knew that to the end of her days in the convent Frances was the only child to bathe alone and naked.

'It will seem strange to you for a while,' their father said. 'You will find it hard at first. But you will be staying here until you finish school, and it will be up to you to make it pleasant or unpleasant, depending on your behaviour.'

Elizabeth said nothing, but Louise, sobbing gently, reminded their father of his wife who had trembled her way into his affection. She had been such a sweet little thing, after all, and so delighted with his praise, so eager for his company. Although she had a Bible – a family Bible, she had called it – the religion thing did not seem to mean very much to her as she never went to church when he knew her first. It was in the family Bible that he read the names, Grace Holderness from her loving mother Elizabeth Gascoyne Holderness, and asked her about them and discovered the landed, newly landless Gascoynes not so far back at all. How would her family, her families, react if she married a Catholic, if she turned, as turn she must? He did not see that the questions meant nothing to her, there were no Gascoynes in her life, her mother was long dead and no one had come from the Holdernesses to relieve her of her meagre office job and spin her away to the Hall and its stables and shooting-parties and church pew. She *had* changed eagerly, confirming herself in his love, marrying quickly, quietly, depending on his sustenance.

'Your mother has gone back to live in England,' he told them. Elizabeth could tell he was lying, looking at his teeth under his black moustache. She was the one who had heard him lie before, before their mother ceased to appease him. She had watched how those many welcomes after his journeys abroad had melted before his discomfort, his haste to be ready for another trip. She had known he was ashamed of them when they all went to Mass together, and Fr Smayle had said, 'You're getting to be quite a stranger, Mrs Galloway,' in that way he had that meant something else, and their father had said wasn't there anything else to put on the girls except the red hand-knitted jerseys which he said, accurately if he meant robins, made them look like birds.

Was it after that lie that Frances stopped looking for the bus with her mother in it? Elizabeth did not know, and never told the other two of her fearful, shameful vigil at the wicket gate in the convent railings, but told them for the years after that they needed to hear it how their mother loved them. Really. How nothing had been her fault – and that was another lie.

'Of course you will miss your mother,' Mr Galloway allowed as he drove them to a restaurant in another town. 'But she is not able to look after you now that you are growing so big. You need to be at school. She could not manage the money and you were not being properly dressed, or properly educated. You never went to Mass.'

'We went to church.' Frances, before Elizabeth could stop her, wanted to put him right. 'We did, Daddy. We went to Mr Craig and I was at Sunday School. I know a lot about the Bible now – I was good.' She thought she could appease him too, and tried, and Louise, trying like the others to be terrifically well-behaved, told him politely that in Mr Craig's churchyard they had found a head-stone with Galloway on it.

'Madeline Gwendolyn Galloway,' recited Louise in her remembering voice. 'Born April 1885, died August 1893: *For he shall give his angels charge over thee, to keep thee in all thy ways.*'

'That's a Protestant church, and you're not Protestants.' Mr Galloway hit on the truth at last. 'You're Catholics, and from now on you're going to a Catholic school and a Catholic church, and you'll be brought up by right-thinking women who know the difference between right and wrong and who know the meaning of sacraments and vows and who'll train you to be good wives and mothers too.'

His vehemence was too much for Frances, who began to cry: 'I want my wife and mother. She's my wife and mother too,' and Louise sat silent beside her, her eyes hunting the pastures outside the car, the fields foaming with daisies.

'Will Mammy come and visit us?' asked Elizabeth, who knew she would make her mother take them all home.

'I don't know,' the answer was quick. 'That's up to her.' But he did know how little of what was up to her Mrs Galloway was capable of doing.

Louise must have understood him, somehow. Once when Elizabeth had grown tired of watching for the green bus, she saw Louise climbing the wall and sitting on the one smooth stone.

'What are you looking out for?' Elizabeth was surprised. She had never seen Louise here before.

'Oh, nothing,' Louise said, straightening her serge skirt over her knees. 'I just thought it's been a while since Daddy came. He might come today. Perhaps I'll see his car on the road.'

'Don't catch cold,' warned Elizabeth, leaving a vigil she would not keep, and indeed Louise did not keep it for long that day, or ever again.

They were not the only girls staying on in the convent when the school-terms ended, although Mother Benignus often advised other parents against letting their children remain during the holidays because they would have the company only of the Galloway girls. But before Sr Margaret Rose became Sr Perpetua the nun was allowed a last visit home and as it was summer time she asked if Frances might be allowed to accompany her.

The yellow farmhouse held on to a slope of foothill, with small fields spraying out from the yards in front and behind. A brief level patch of land at the side of the steep house had been given over to an orchard where apples grew with blackcurrants and loganberries, and all the south-facing windows in the house had their inside ledges studded with ripening tomatoes. There had been too many children in that household for Frances to be made a stranger; the girl of the moment was Margaret Rose, and around her a complex drama began to weave as soon as she got out of the bus in the village and into her father's trap, the only conveyance of the kind Frances had ever seen and which was one of the many uncomplicated delights of her visit.

It was the time for making hay, but Margaret Rose had no work of that kind to do, staying instead in the kitchen by day to make the cakes, to cook the huge hams and coils of cold grey beef which emerged, glistening and red and pungent with salt from the huge pans on the range. When the boys and their father came in they brought other men, and in the long evenings they sat indoors and out, and the air filled with pipe and cigarette smoke and the girls and women from other farms, from the village, came up to talk and to drink stout and sherry and port and later, when most of the women were gone, the unnamed white liquid that made people gasp and swear.

Frances fitted into this life like a drop of water into a well. She slept in a truckle bed and rose with the first light, lingering in her room only to savour the adult delight of being alone. In the kitchen she was allowed to turn her hand to anything that came her way, frying the thick chunks of bread for the early breakfasts or making up a feed for the hens, to every one of which she had given a name within a day of seeing them. She picked fruit in the orchard, and topped and tailed the yellow and red gooseberries while sitting on the wall of flat stones outside the house. The father and brothers of Margaret Rose were quiet, undemonstrative men, but one of them – afterwards she always insisted to herself that his name was Thady – had shyly brought her a piece of honeycomb, its golden juice running among the dark green bubbles of a cabbage leaf. At noon she carried baskets with Margaret Rose down to the groups of men in the fields, napkins covering piles of bread and meat, scones pitted with currants, cans of steaming tea, tall tin jugs of milk, and in the evening when the pale deal table in the kitchen was dressed with the hams, the chickens, the bowls as big as cradles of potatoes, it was her task to stand on the wall beyond the front door and wave a white tablecloth so that they would all come home together. Margaret Rose's mother presided at these feasts with the same genial calm she beamed when standing over the washtub or directing the plunging streams of milk from the patient cows in the byre. Frances had had a feeling that there was something rude about this intimate contact with the animal teat, but when she tried it herself and felt the silk skin yield to her grasp and the milky stream begin to flow, she flushed with the pleasure of success and discovered innocent sensuality.

The entire family went to Mass together, the women making the journey in the trap pulled by the vigorous brown pony Frances had learned to pet. There were many ponies and carts at the church gates, a few round cars as well, and inside, the cool church sweated with people aching to be out of doors once more. The priest was small and fat and hot and tossed Latin on the marble altar alight with flowers and candles, and preached a sermon about the foreign missions as quickly as he could. Fasting from the night before and now accustomed to a hearty breakfast Frances felt thin with hunger when she went to the altar-rails with Margaret Rose. While the host melted on her tongue her thoughts were all of sausages and tomatoes and the bread and gooseberry jam there would be later on; as they left the church in a crowd, one of the boys – it must have been Thady, Frances always said later – pushed a hard square of chocolate into her hand and told her in a whisper to eat it quick before the others would want a bit.

Was it that night, a Sunday night, that was Margaret Rose's last night at home? Forever? The carts and cars came toiling to the front yard, and girls in hard bright clothes with careful hair brought whispered stories to an end when they saw the men coming up. Old women sat in the cool parlour, always known as 'the room' and sipped sherry and were often silent, but the men filled the kitchen and flowed out, young and old, to the airy yard where the girls began to leave their clutter around Margaret Rose and talked lightly about going for a little walk, the evening was so fine. As the couples strayed away and back and changed their partners, a fiddle was brought out and the laments of the valley were offered to the night.

The square swept yard and the flagged kitchen left room for jigs and reels from the old men whose polished boots twisted upon each other as they stepped it out, and the girls and boys whopped through the circles of the set dances, 'The Walls of Limerick', *Casadh an tSúgan*. The sweet wild violin rested while an accordion gave waltzes and a reason, even in front of the hot little priest who had walked up on his own, for the young people to touch one another, to hold and cling and confide in the dying light of the day.

Margaret Rose waltzed too, her brothers and cousins swirling her in their arms, but she grew quiet after just a few dances and sat closer to her mother and father, and to Frances who had moved from wall to door, to window-sill, watching, marking, making it all her own. The mother's face had seemed to Frances to be thinner in these past days, she had been more silent. Frances saw the father's skin burn deeper, not just with the sun, with the reddening that had made his eyes look wet and his mouth tucked in more firmly.

A light boyish tenor carried a tune in from the yard:

> 'From this valley they say you are going,
> We shall miss your bright eyes and sweet smile,
> For they say you are taking the sunshine
> That brightened our pathways a while.'

A net of voices lifted the song, young voices, the old farmers and villagers and their wives were silent, this was not how they would sing:

> 'Come and sit by my side if you love me,
> Do not hasten to bid me adieu
> But remember the Red River Valley,
> And the cowboy who loved you so true.'

Louise sang often in the convent, one result of a decision taken, now that the girls were getting older and really quite well-behaved, to let them visit the nuns' holiday house in Ardmore.

'Picture!' Sr Perpetua said when Elizabeth told her of the plan.

'You'll be able to swim there, on the nuns' beach: I'll ask Reverend Mother about bathing costumes for you all.'

The square grey house held wonders for them, not least that of seeing nuns from other houses of the sisterhood, not least from watching them at their idea of fun, the more daring producing surreptitious packs of cards, the more kind inviting the girls to join in games of Lotto and Ludo. Their yellow stretch of sand lay with its back to the curve of cardboard dwellings which daily issued streamers of loud-voiced frantic children. Encouraged to ignore all that billowing, bellowing activity the three girls walked instead among the stone cottages of the village, the painted houses terracing the hill above the exciting sea. The nuns had a boat and a boatman and one evening they rowed up to Monatrea on the narrowing Blackwater, the crowded cloudy woods darkening as they returned, the river smell giving way to the tang of the open sea whose waves drove in on them as the little boat lifted on the swell.

Lulled as they had been by their exploration of the old Abbey ruins, nuns and children alike had drifted into an easy silence on the journey home, but now the choppy tilt of the vessel roused them, the shores laden with drowsy trees faded away from the nimbus of the widening bay. The ocean lay before them, and Elizabeth looked again at the slide of water in the bottom of the boat, measuring. The soft little nun from County Meath who had been teaching the girls to swim began to sing – 'Speed, bonny boat, like a bird on the wing' – and the other nuns joined in, the lurching rhythm catching the pull of the oars against the tide. Hearing the words, finding the lilt, Louise blended her voice with the singing voices and left the chorale to raise the song in a harmony of her own, offering a gliding flock of notes to the sudden, smiling stars. The squat lighthouse at Youghal beamed out as the boat crunched on their beach, and even the nuns who could not sing sang as the boatman, his own voice laughing in the night, helped them to jump over the rippled waves that lay against the shore.

Sr Perpetua said she was amazed when Louise told her about joining the school choir. Sr Mary Columbanus had said she was good enough, and her father had been asked to allow a new uniform for the public concert in the hall.

'Picture!' Elizabeth and Frances had said together, folding themselves in giggles and satire, as Louise paraded her new ribbons, perched like grosgrain butterflies on either side of her rosy, satisfied face. Sr Perpetua struggled with the unruly hair which would not stay restrained into plaits, and the unaccustomed children did not recognise the pride in her gaze when she looked at Louise in her finery of serge and poplin.

There must have been some tremor of pride, too, in Mr Galloway, for he sent them money for the first time.

'Money each?' wondered Frances, looking at the green notes in Elizabeth's hand.

'Money each,' Elizabeth said, not telling them how much, giving a single pound to Frances, a pound and ten shillings to Louise, keeping two pounds and ten shillings for herself.

'It's for the concert,' Elizabeth explained. 'For the stalls and sweets and things. You can buy what you like.'

It was a Saturday, a brisk winter morning with the school thumping with battened excitement, a feeling of hurried informality, of freedom. On the bus taking her to Mallow, and then on to Cork, Elizabeth breathed a cold consciousness of what she was doing; not running away, running towards. Finding. Answering that letter which spoke of Alton's Shop, South Terrace, care of. Underneath the chill of the adventure ran the hot current of desperation which had cooled into her intention, and hardened. Already skilful at subterfuge it had not been difficult to leave the school, to make herself inconspicuous on the bus, the right bus too.

The mist from the frosted fields yielded to the sunlight as the journey went on, the country outside the windows glistened as if new. The morning sky looked thin and pink as if it had been peeled, and the woods around Blarney floated in brown and purple clouds above the town, the great square keep of the castle standing bare to Elizabeth's searching eyes. The twisting road unrolled towards the city, heralded by sea-gulls and steeples, and at the terminus Elizabeth was baffled by bridges. She asked her way; there was nothing to remark in her teenage demeanour, her queries gave no hint of anxiety, she was shown her route without comment.

Benign everywhere else, at the South Terrace the sun turned ugly. Gaunt houses with small-windowed attics peering from their roofs stood hard on the uneven pavements, and the stepped white planks from the timber-yard looked raw against the walls. Alton's shop hid around a corner, its window forlorn with forgotten notices, and inside there was the thick compound smell of cheese and yellow cakes and coal-dust and paraffin. A fat man with a loose lower lip glowered at Elizabeth's question.

'Mrs Galloway? Know her, do ye? We haven't seen her here – and we'd like to, we'd like to. Tell her that – Johnny Alton'd like to see her.'

To see him, purple-faced and repulsive, spitting contempt for her mother, was the first shock of this journey for Elizabeth. In the street again she looked wildly around, disoriented and afraid. In her pocket she had enough money to get back to the school if she had to go back, that was not her fear. What gripped her was the loneliness of her concentration; what if the centre of her heart were not to be found? It was almost a year since she had last seen her mother, there had been months between each stolen meeting, encounters with no joy, offering nothing except continuity, a link with what had once been her life, their lives. This search assumed that the continuity was rooted, that her mother came to Elizabeth from a place in which their lives could thrive again. It was hope, no more; now Elizabeth faced despair.

Cracked steps led to an open door, gaping into a littered,

cavernous hall. By asking and asking Elizabeth had found a possible person; maybe her mother was the English lady in number 16. Her second thumping knock on the door, the lead knocker falling heavily from her hand to the peeling timber, produced a voice at least, and that voice high and uncertain and known.

The woman with greying hair looked at the girl.

'Elizabeth?' There were no outstretched arms, no tears of joy, 'What in the name of God are you doing here? You must go back, go back at once!'

The hall echoed to her voice, the startled words glancing off the stairs and ceiling. Elizabeth had expected surprise but no anger, and she heard anger in the echoes. The elation of her success vanished. She became very young again, she could not speak.

'Oh God, what am I to do with you now? You must go back, you must!'

A call, thick and male, came through the vault of the stairs: 'Lally? What are you doing down there? What's going on?'

Mrs Galloway looked at Elizabeth sadly. The girl had shivered as she heard the shouted name. Lally. Her mother's pet name. She had no memory, now, of her father ever using it. It had been theirs, held between the mother and her daughters, theirs only.

'You'd better come up. It's freezing here.'

Climbing the stairs after her, Elizabeth saw how the trousers fell like bags from her mother's bones. The grimy light falling through the landings as they mounted showed her face older, worn, without the flush of secrecy. Her hair was still long, but falling from its metal grips at the back and almost colourless, its blackness faded and wan, its dull fringe stranded with grey.

Elizabeth had no sense of her own self; no idea of how, to her mother, she looked tall and firm with health, bright with the colours of youth. Cared for, if not cared about.

A strong bewitching smell met Elizabeth; in a cluttered room a fire burned eagerly, and the man standing by the hearth, a glass frothing in his hand, was laughing as he looked at her.

'Who's this, then? One of your sprats?'

Through his beard his lips were very red.

'This is our all, young lady. We've no place to put you – unless you want to squeeze between Lally and me on the bed?'

It was a joke, but a brutal one to the girl. She had seen the brass bed with its tumbled coloured covers, the man's clothes on the hook on the wall. The window had no curtains, and beside its light an easel stood firm, a table nearby held tubes and pots, brushes stood on end with pencils and black sticks, there were hues and textures everywhere, fabric, substance. Only Mrs Galloway looked bleached.

'What will I do with her? She's run away from school.'

'Send her back. There's nothing else for it. Pity and all that, Lally, but she can't stay here.'

It was happening to Elizabeth. It was happening, as it had happened before, but this time she had invited it. She was dumb with the disaster.

Drinking his beer, the man explained.

'Couldn't keep you even if we had the room. We're packing up here, going off. To England, where I can sell my work. Art has no place in Ireland, these days – ever get out of that convent of yours, to a museum, a gallery? Of course not!'

He was not indignant. Elizabeth thought through his words

to the pink and white plaster statue of the Virgin in the school hall, the great bleeding crucifix in the church, the Stations of the Cross.

'We have a lot of statues and pictures,' she said at last, stung to defence. 'And we have art. Art classes. Sr Bonaventure takes us for art and physical education.'

'Oh, that's it all right, art and physical education.' The sneer went out of his tone: 'Like it, do you? The school? Like being with your sisters?'

Elizabeth could not tell him of her need. She could not tell either how she knew about the passage of time, that for her before too long there would be decisions, departures, a life after school.

To her silence he said: 'Better to stick it out. Education always has a price on it, and at the end of this you'll be educated. That's a lot, you know. And in the meantime – food, shelter, clothing, company; is it so bad? What more could anyone want?'

Mrs Galloway handed him another bottle of beer and Elizabeth looked at him, the cold light trembling as it warmed by the fire, how he stood in it at ease, his life around him but portable, the woman waiting.

'My mother,' she began, unconsciously talking to him, as if Mrs Galloway were not there. The woman moved from her stand by the fire, uneasy.

'I came to see my mother. That's all. We had a free day at school and I had the money so I came to see her. I'm going back on the next bus. It is all right.'

Something from her tight distress must have reached Mrs Galloway. She took coins from a plate on the mantelpiece.

'Here – a few bob for the trip. Button your coat up now,

it's so cold. I'll walk to the bus with you, and you can tell me about the girls.'

In the street Mrs Galloway said: 'He looked after me, Elizabeth, when I was in trouble. You can't know about all the things that have happened to me. Try not to think badly of me. Please.'

'It's all right,' Elizabeth said politely. 'I only came to see you. I thought, when I leave school, I should know where you live. That's all. It's all right.'

They waited in a long silence for the bus, sitting in the shabby terminus in the comfortless cold. People shuffled around them, herded between tannoy and notice-board. Poor people, country people, with sacking bags spilling intimacies.

Squalid, Elizabeth realised. This is squalid, it is sordid, this whole place, this whole thing. Her mother too. 'Lally!' she said fiercely to herself. 'Lally!' and her fury broke into anguish and Lally sitting beside her saw tears spout from her daughter's desperate eyes.

'I'll have to go now,' she whispered sharply. 'Stop crying, nothing is any worse than it was.'

Elizabeth's sobs were loud, helpless.

'Stop it.' Mrs Galloway had risen. 'Please, darling, do stop it. I must go, people are looking at us. Don't worry about me, I'll be all right. Oh, do stop crying, Elizabeth. Goodbye. I have to go – I must!'

People thought the girl was distressed at parting, and explained her tears kindly to one another. They shepherded Elizabeth onto the bus, and at each halt on the long final journey there were gentle words and reminders, a knowing generous feeling for the disablement of grief.

Dark came down on the country like a blanket falling slowly on flame, and Elizabeth saw through drying eyes how the small lights of houses came through the blackness, their chill radiance as distant as the stars. The convent was bright, brimming with sound and life as she fitted herself into the back row of the school hall, among classmates who had noticed her absence without wondering.

She was in time for the choir, Louise's choir; they sang in Irish the song about Kilcash, the lament for a life that was lost, the house and its lady no more. '*Cad a dheanfaimid feasta gan adhmad?*' What shall we do for timber now, the last of the woods have fallen? What shall we do for timber, Elizabeth thought, searching for shelter from the loss of her life.

Frances found her.

'We knew you were gone. We didn't tell anyone. Only Sr Perpetua, because she came looking for you at tea-time. But Louise told a lie, and it's all right. Where were you? Where did you go?'

With her money she had bought a book about an English boarding school – *Dimsie*; apples and sweets and a lace-edged handkerchief of white cotton with a satin rose in the corner, an E for Elizabeth stitched around the flower.

'It's for you. E for Elizabeth. I was thinking of you. Where did you go to?'

Louise too had thought of Elizabeth, lying quickly and efficiently when required, although perhaps Sr Perpetua had not believed her.

'But she's such a pet she won't tell, not now you've come back. Where did you go?'

'I went to Cork.' Elizabeth saw their eyes round, their mouths open. 'I thought I knew where Mummy would be.'

MARY LELAND

There was a luminosity in their faces. They loved this adult
Elizabeth, who was daring, and brave on their behalf. They
shone with excited hope.

Elizabeth shook her head.

'No. She wasn't there. I thought I knew, but I tried there
and they said she was gone. Gone to England. And then I
came home.'

Although the hope was gone, the excitement was still
there, the energy of the adventure. Frances wanted more,
the details, the bus, the people, the shops. She would live
on it for months. Louise saw some outline of a disaster, but
said only, 'So, Daddy was right. Remember, he told us she
was gone back to England.'

'Oh, yes,' Elizabeth agreed. 'Daddy was right.'

The years after that explained many of the mysteries to the
girls, although not in order, or in due time. Where there
were no explanations, understanding came instead, slowly.

'Perhaps it would have been better if we had been boys –
better for Daddy, I mean,' pondered Frances. After his funeral
Elizabeth had left her teacher-training college to deal with
solicitors, her first object being the release of her sisters
from the convent. It had puzzled and hurt her that they did
not want to go, not before time.

'Still, he left us all he had,' said Louise, who at last was
learning to be a singer. 'He must have wanted to do that,
wanted us to have what he had, whether we were boys or
girls. Boys might have satisfied his pride or something, but
he would still have had to do something about us, or them,
you know what I mean. I mean, there would still have been
a problem.'

'Anyway,' Elizabeth said, always the pragmatist, 'he didn't

90

have any choice in the matter. We were all he had, so he had to leave it to us. We were his heirs.'

'Heiresses,' corrected Frances at last at University.

'Heiresses,' said Elizabeth, not thinking at all of the room in Cork with its smell of turpentine, its brass bed.

'And I will never understand why he hated us.' Frances had decided that he did, a long time ago.

'What I will never understand,' said Elizabeth, 'is why *they* hated us. The nuns.'

'Ah, they didn't all hate us,' said Louise, thinking of the glory of music. 'Not Sr Mary Columbanus; she taught me to sing, she liked to hear me singing. I think she liked me.'

'And not Sr Perpetua,' said Frances, looking at the newspaper with Lady Elizabeth Holderness and the Gascoyne Trophy. 'Not Sr Perpetua.' And her fingers lightly outlined the shape and shadows of the picture.

VAL MULKERNS

Summer

S arah's flight had not yet been called and there was plenty of time. Her baggage checked in, she was deep now in a fashion magazine, blue-jeaned knees together and feet spread wide. She looked as carelessly uninvolved as though she were sitting on the floor of her chaotic room at home.

'Have you your passport safely stowed away?'

'Oh, Mother, you saw me do it at the check-in.'

'Did you actually *take* the Kwells? I last noticed them in your hand.'

'I actually took the Kwells. Look, relax. I have my francs and my traveller's cheques and my separate embarkation fee. I have your presents for the Vendrons (whenever I see them) and twenty changes of socks. It's not my first flight and I haven't failed my entire exam, just Structures like everybody else. I won't jump out of the plane as we take off and I won't crunch up all the travel pills. I won't die of dysentery and I'm unlikely to fall into the hands of a really competent rapist. You should know by now I'm better able to take care of myself than you are and I'm delirious to be escaping. There, they're calling my flight. Number 8 gate.'

Magazine tucked into the big canvas shoulder-bag, she stood tall and smiling down at Emily, clean black hair falling around her narrow face, eyes already away and somewhere else. On the escalator she bent and laid her cheek, moist and cool as a fruit, against Emily's.

'There isn't anywhere in the world I'd rather be going. Your fault. You made me a Francophile before I left my pram. You taught me "Frère Jacques" when you should have been teaching me ABC. You exchanged me for a Vendron at the tender age of twelve and I've never been more terrified in my life than on that first plane flying off alone into the unknown.'

'You were being met at Le Bourget.'

'Yes, but I didn't believe it. I didn't believe I'd live so long, and I wanted to howl like an infant and beg you to call it all off and let me live shamefully ever after.'

'You looked so cool,' Emily remembered. She had believed all the turmoil was inside herself. The forlornness of the school blazer. The smallness of Sarah as she had stumped across the tarmac, handgrip held in both arms like a puppy. Yet a few minutes previously she had kissed them coldly goodbye, exchanged a few giggling jokes with her friends who had stayed the night to be in time to see her off. All of eight years ago.

'Tell Denis when he gets back,' she said carefully at the gate. 'Tell him I said goodbye.' At the age of three Sarah had called her mother Emily but had reverted soon afterwards to custom. Her father had always remained Denis. 'Tell him

93

thanks for the money and I'll write – well, some time. Tell him, won't you?'

'I'll tell him. And I hope the job turns out to be interesting. I wouldn't mind being in your shoes myself.'

'Why don't you come?' Eyes wide open in the hard-worked pale face, Sarah really seemed to mean it.

'Don't be silly. Give the Vendrons my love – especially Nathalie.'

'Of course, though I may not see much of them. Thanks for the lift, Mother, and the money and everything. And I will write – promise.'

'Ask them over for Christmas if they'd like to come.'

'Perhaps. But you know their position about the grandmother. Goodbye Mother.'

'Goodbye, love. Bon voyage.' They kissed briefly.

Due to the new security regulations you couldn't go any further, but by good fortune she caught sight of Sarah ten minutes afterwards, swinging long-legged across the tarmac, cheese-cloth smock about to take off by itself, it seemed, in the strong wind. Sarah was among the tallest of the hurrying passengers and there was about her an air of joyful freedom, from study, from Dublin, naturally from home. The small squat creature in the school blazer had gone bravely to her doom. In one sense she had never come back.

Denis had stood too and watched the plane take off that first time, a great menacing bird with flames at its tail. They had not admitted to feeling sick with worry, but Denis had taken her hand and squeezed it fiercely. She stood alone now on the balcony waiting for take-off. The warm wind got inside her cotton dress, lifting it free, as she made her ritual wordless prayer for a safe arrival. Sarah was beyond her care now, a woman with the right to the wrong decisions so long as they were her own. She imagined the pale bony face tilted back in the seat, the capable bony hands fixing the seat belt, hands that could sketch, paint, make detailed plans for houses she might never build, cook, sew, and no doubt make love.

The plane was ready now. The crew had gone aboard and now the pilot mounted the steps with a nod of thanks to the men who had fuelled his engines. Sarah was in the care of other people. For ever now. Emily watched the flames, saw the plane which had taxied toy-like around the runway shudder into flight and climb steeply into a grey June sky. She waved as Sarah was perhaps invisibly waving. Bon voyage.

Brown-stained fingers had pressed into her arm that first time. 'She's beginning her independence. Already detached from us, already chatting to strangers on either side of her. She's safe and happy and being met at Le Bourget. She doesn't even remember that we exist any more. Come and have a drink.'

Shakily they had drunk without words to Sarah's safety, Sarah's happiness, Sarah's proficiency at French. The two friends with school blazers like Sarah's had sucked their Coke warily through straws, a little lost now that Sarah was gone. At home in the suddenly empty house she and Denis had made urgent love before he went to work, one of the few completely spontaneous occasions she could remember. It had ended in laughter because the cat had been under the bed and squawked at the rustling springs before leaping out onto the window sill. Sunshine through the open window. The blinking black cat. A lawnmower whirring somewhere. I love you.

On the way home from the airport she dropped in on friends who (she had forgotten) were away on holiday. She spent an hour at a deplorable annual Academy exhibition in the National Gallery and had lunch there; a wandering afternoon in town followed. Twice she went into a public phone box and stood irresolute, the phone poised. When you didn't ring I thought perhaps you were ill again so I decided to check. How are you? No. It was over. She put back the receiver, preferring not to hear that cautious voice inventing the customary lies. It had been good and it was over and no harm done unless she made a fool of herself now. During a heavy shower she went into a cinema and stayed although she had seen the film before. It hadn't been worth anybody's time in the first place. She had another cup of coffee somewhere else and finally home could not be put off any longer. There was a letter on the kitchen table.

> Emily, I'm unlikely to be back early. Hope Sarah went off OK and that she didn't forget anything vital. Thanks for the salmon I found in the fridge. I've somehow remembered to order a pint less milk for tomorrow but I could find no food for the cat. You should turn in early after all the rush of getting Sarah off. Try this Lionel Davidson − I liked it. D.

The note was under the paperback. It was half past eleven and still not quite dark in the garden. A warm breath of fading hawthorn came through the open window. She saw herself reflected in the glass, the note from Denis in one hand, his book in the other. This was the time Sarah would sometimes come running along the hall upstairs when she'd let herself in after the last bus. They would make coffee in the kitchen and turn over the news of the day. Jer and Catherine had broken it off again. Fergus had walked out on the parents and was sleeping rough in Stephen's Green. His old dear had recently started to open his letters and sniff around for drugs. She was too stupid to know that what she ought to be sniffing around for was bombs.

The old cat rubbed against Emily's ankles, bundled clumsily across the tiles to the empty bowl and back again to her ankles. Denis had been right – there was no cat food in the fridge. She had forgotten to get it at the butcher's yesterday. Maybe a saucer of milk would do. No. The furry collision with her ankles began all over again, a rasping of the tongue against her bare flesh, the clumsy journey back again to the milk-filled bowl. So far the creature was not howling; that would come later. Sighing, she fetched a slice of bacon from the fridge and cut it up with the kitchen scissors but that too was rejected, so there was only one thing to do. Hurriedly she gathered into a saucepan a heap of unpicked chicken bones. Since they had been reserved for soup anyway there was nothing to lose by simmering them now instead of tomorrow and there was supper to gain for the cat who knew this routine and had now given up demanding instant food. It sat at her elbow as she opened the book, making its wheezy attempt at purring.

Tired of the sound, she wandered upstairs to run a bath. Idly stepping into Sarah's room while the bath filled, she saw herself once again reflected in the blank window above the dark garden and because she didn't like what she saw she quickly pulled across the curtains. The room smelled more than ever of Sarah, of youth. Yellow lamplight showed her the chaotic disorder, maddening when Sarah was at home, childlike and touching now that she was gone.

Rejected garments for the suitcase overflowed from the open chest of drawers, littered the bed, joined a jumble on the floor of text books, sketch books, hair rollers, paper patterns, snippets of the new summer frocks she had made in the last few days, a half-eaten Mars bar and an unused tampon. The window seat was completely obscured by similar litter including shoes, boots and sandals as though they had been deliberately laid out the way a child lays out coloured sweets for selection. Compulsively Emily began to make order, interrupting the job once to turn off the bath water, then returning to sift, discard or rearrange the litter of Sarah's life.

'*Soyez réaliste,*' she had written across the cover of a big sketch book, '*demandez l'impossible.*' Not only did Sarah ask the impossible but sometimes she did it. It was during the week before one of her examinations that she had made a summer dress for Emily's birthday. No snippet of cotton had appeared anywhere to suggest what was to come, no piece of paper pattern had been left to give the game away. A blue cotton dress perfectly finished to the last detail and a perfect fit had been dumped one morning into her arms before Sarah banged the door and raced away to a lecture for which she was already late.

Inside a college magazine called *Structures* there was a sheet of paper that drifted free as Emily gathered all the magazines together:

> Arm-strapped together we watched up west
> The blood of murdered day breaking night's rest.

Motorbikes. The boy whose fledgling effort this was used to come surrounded by them as Aengus was by birds. He didn't own a motorbike but he collected friends who did. That summer motorbikes crowded for ever on the bare patch they had made under the trees. Indoors Simon and Garfunkel and the buzz of voices after school, Sarah's room overflowing onto the stairs. A pong of Gauloises or perhaps pot. Coffee and 'Bridge Over Troubled Waters'. Shouts of laughter. Always more boys than girls. The one who wrote the poem also fed the cat while they were away on that last family holiday. Because he loved cats he had come in every day for a month and he had sent on selected post also. The house had not felt empty when they came home. He was a big brown curly bear of a boy – what was his name? Ruairí. He had left a note with the month's bills on the kitchen table.

Ah ah! Don't look. One suspects a predominance of canondal mordentary apperatures. Anyway they all arrived too late to send on except 2 which were filed in my impeccable system under W for 'Where do I put these?' Céad mile fáilte (approx equal to 400 new fáiltes) Cheers. Ruairí.

The note fluttered out with the poem and the closing fragment of a letter. 'But me no goodbyes. Parting is such sweet whatyacallit. Brightness falls into the lair. Give you good morrow. Your sleepless step-in wolf.'

He was dead two years now, found a tangle of bones and burnt metal when he crashed a borrowed motorbike one Saturday night on the Bray Road. These pages Sarah had kept together were evidently a memorial collection. But me no goodbyes. Parting is such sweet whatyacallit.

*   *   *

Sarah's sheets were rumpled but changing them would have seemed like rejection. They smelled of lemon soap and patchouli and made a warmer bed than the one upstairs. After a bath she was reading Sarah's Tolkien and half asleep when a key turned in the hall door. Switching off the light was instinctive but sleep was now far away. A smell of burnt bones crept up from the kitchen and already the heavy footsteps of Denis were sounding from that direction. He would find a starving beast and a ruin of spoiled supper. She began to laugh with hysterical guilt and then put her head under the clothes to stifle the sound. Faintly she could hear the yowls of the cat in panic-stricken welcome and her mind followed Denis's movements. First things first. He would switch off the cooker. Then open windows and doors wide. Then comfort the afflicted animal. Most probably he would make such a determined effort that he would find the cat something apart from the piece of uncooked salmon in the fridge. She had one impulse to go down and make abject apologies but in a little while this impulse was completely conquered. Tomorrow would be time enough.

She woke next morning to a silent house and sun flooding through the curtains. The house felt empty, which was impossible. Downstairs, nevertheless, it was empty, with a note on the kitchen table to prove it.

Emily, I'm afraid you forgot the chicken bones again. Cleared up as best I could and found a tin of cat food out in the car – dating from that camping holiday years ago, I have no doubt. It seemed quite fresh however and the cat didn't complain. You were sleeping so soundly I didn't like to waken you to let you know I must put in a few hours work to make up for a broken day yesterday when I had to see Henderson. Appointment with the Minister on Monday morning and practically no background data prepared. May not get home for lunch so don't wait. D.

Working on Sundays was something new but then his partner was on holiday. If Denis could find the slightest excuse for extra work he wouldn't hesitate. She wanted to ring him and apologise, say something to hear him laugh. But there was nobody on the switchboard. Even if she drove into the main entrance the office block would be closed to everybody who hadn't a private key – he might as well be on the moon.

She opened the windows wide and hoped the reek of burnt bones would go away in the sunshine. Leaning out on the window sill she sniffed the morning. Hawthorn still, and wild garlic, and a hint of tom cats. In a moment there was the creak of a basket behind her and the huge woolly creature walked stiff-legged across the tiles. Its fur in the sunlight was a decayed brownish black, profuse because of remote Persian ancestry. Its golden goat's eyes avoided her when it lumbered up on the window sill. Nevertheless it sat companionably by her elbow and yawned, diffusing its old cat smell.

Mechanically she stroked it, and its strange rattling purr grew louder.

It was so old that it had curled up beside Sarah in the cot, guarding her from wasps in summer and from boredom at all times. Its name was Simpkin and Denis claimed that some vital mechanism (like the gizzard of a goose) had stopped working inside so that the cat had no way of dealing with the accumulation of fur swallowed during its ablutions. That is, it had one way, recently devised. Sometimes Emily would find a ball of fur and mucus near its basket on the tiles and for a few days it would sound less wheezy before the fur built up again. Eventually she supposed it would choke and then they could keep a dog instead.

It licked her wrist now with a rasping tongue before lumbering over the window sill into the garden. All old creatures, animal and human, move in the same way. Simpkin in bright incongruous sunshine looked more than somewhat like Aunt Harry. It was Sunday. 'Just as soon as I pack Sarah off I'll be over to see you,' she remembered saying. Sarah was wakening up in Paris or already sitting on the balcony, drinking café au lait out of a big bowl, apricot jam heaped into a split roll on her plate. There isn't anywhere in the world I'd rather be going, Sarah had said. But this was Dublin and today was Harry's day. Turning on her heel to make coffee, Emily found herself sliding on the tiles and bent down to see why. The ball of mucus and fur had been silently left at her feet, like an offering.

MARY BECKETT

Under Control

My dear Peggy,

The other day my next-door neighbour told me about a quarrel with her sister as a result of which she wrote a letter, twenty-five pages long, to her daughter doing a Ph.D in Seattle, Washington. Here I am writing this to my sister married in Oxford about my daughter who will never get a Ph.D in Seattle or anywhere else. Why do I burden you with this? I remember when Mother told me about her worries I used to say to myself, 'Why does she pile it all on me? What's wrong with her talking to Father?' I normally talk things over with Owen, you know that, but, when I see the looks of dislike that he gives his beloved daughter nowadays, I can't say a word to him about her. I know you love her and will be able to separate fact from reality in what I tell you. And she loves you far more than she does me. 'Do you know how much I hate you?' she asked me this morning. It was no shock to me, but I didn't like to hear it said. I told her I knew she didn't like me and that it was a pity because I loved her, always loved her, that she was especially dear to me, being our first baby after the little one that died. She told me then that I was telling lies, that I never thought much of her, that I'd hated her since before Susan was born.

I know you're thinking that with Susan two years old now we should all have adapted to the way things have turned out, but a letter came on the morning's post – an anonymous letter. It threatened that Susan's mother, having realised that I was above the legal age to be given a child to adopt, was going to apply to the Courts to have Susan returned to her. I can't think who wrote it. I haven't given my mind to that yet. Stella was still at the breakfast table in her dressing-gown, face not washed, hair not brushed. I can never get her out in time for her early lectures. I handed her the letter and said, 'She's got hold of the wrong end of the stick, hasn't she?' Maybe it wasn't the most tactful thing to say but it always amuses me the way they question me about my letters – who wrote that, what has she to say, who are you writing to? It's the same with telephone calls, in spite of our giving them perfect privacy. We never say, 'What time were you in at last night?' but if I stop to talk to somebody coming home from the church there is a real inquisition. 'Where were you? Why were you not home long ago? What did you find to talk about so long?' That's why I handed over the letter, although indeed it's more Brian and David that want to keep me circumscribed. Stella doesn't take much interest any more. I try to be careful with her but it's impossible to weigh every word all the time.

She read it and gave it back and that's when she said did I know how much she hated me, that I had never given her any chance of making her own decisions, that I never stopped pushing her, that I had taken her child from her without giving her any option. Did I realise that St Augustine said the chief urge in us is to dominate and that I had never controlled that? She's studying philosophy in university so she throws this at me. Do you, living in Oxford, ever hear any chit-chat about St Augustine and what he said, and what qualifications he has that we should heed anything he did say? Or do the physicists you move among not really care a lot about St Augustine? Perhaps that strange Torus of their concentrates their thoughts so that they have no ideas outside their task of seeking to create power by nuclear fusion rather than fission.

Did Stella ever tell you how she came to have the baby? She's fond of you and must be grateful to you – maybe she told you before now what she told me this morning. 'Told' is not a proper verb to describe her onslaught on me. She was shouting, yelling, until I warned her she'd waken Susan. All the time she looked at me with such detestation that I have to offload it. It's hard for me at this moment to remember the quiet polite girl Stella was all through school, no trouble to anyone and the nuns always telling me she was responsible and co-operative and that it didn't matter at all that her exam results were very mediocre. I used to think she was content – happy would be too strong a word. She didn't go out much, no dances, no boyfriends. I hoped going to the university would improve that but she just stayed with her schoolfriends and worried about her notes and her exams and her money. She was anxious to get a summer job so as to have her own money for the next year and when she got one in a kind of youth hotel in France we were all delighted. I thought it would help her French. She tells me now that I pushed her into taking it just to improve her French, that she was terrified going and that she was killed with loneliness while she was there and what she really wanted was to get into a shop or an office here at home. Her wicked mother threw her out of the nest and she hadn't spoken to a soul all the fortnight she was there before the Friday she telephoned us to find out if she had passed her first-year exams. She hadn't, you remember. Owen had gone over to the university and found that her name was not on the list of passes, but we didn't know how many subjects she had failed and wouldn't until Monday, so we hadn't rung her and hoped she wouldn't ring us, but she did, after dinner-time, and I had to tell her. I remember consoling her with the assurance that she'd get her repeat exams in September, that she should stay where she was until she heard how many subjects she had to repeat. This morning she said that I ordered her to stay where she was, that she'd just have to pass in September or she wouldn't be acceptable at home. She wanted to give up university, she says. She never wanted to go to university. She didn't enjoy studying. She was never any good at it. She hated not doing well in exams when Brian and David were so clever. All she wanted was to get a job and enjoy her own money and her freedom from books. But I was so determined to control her, to push her into things she had no wish for, that she had no chance to run her own life, so she just had the baby to force some change.

She had gone into the nearest town before dark because she was too depressed to stay in her room. By a strange chance she met a lad she'd known to see in college but not to speak to. He was cock-a-hoop because he had passed his final law exams and since he had nobody to celebrate with they went off together and ended up in his bed. When she went back to the hostel she scrubbed herself all over in disgust – every place he had touched, her teeth, her tongue, in horror of herself. Still, on Monday after she rang home and found out she had failed only French and I was insistent that she'd have no difficulty passing one subject in September, the only way out she could think of was to go back to this lad every evening for a week until he moved off to Switzerland. Now you may think this was confiding in me, but not if you'd heard her. It was as if I had arranged for her violation.

I had never allowed myself to wonder how or when it happened. That would have been like reading a diary or her letters. Owen used to say many a time before the baby was born, 'Did she ever tell you how she came to do such a thing?' and I always said no but that I supposed it was because of loneliness, human nature and the skimpy clothes they wore in the heat. They certainly were not in love although maybe Stella was a bit dazzled by him. When she told him in September that she was pregnant he said he took no responsibility, that he was going on for the bar and could have no blemish on his character, and if she said anything he'd deny ever having spoken to her in his life. But you know that. It's all very well for her to say now that she deliberately decided to change her life, but I remember the pathetic picture she made when she told me just afterwards. She didn't know what to do, so it was as well I did in spite of all her talk of my being so domineering. And of course we couldn't have managed if you hadn't been living in England and prepared to take her until after the baby was born. How does any woman manage without a sister? I sometimes feel if our first baby had lived she would have made a difference to Stella. She could have confided in a sister earlier about her irritation with me and her rancour might not have grown into this hatred she feels for me now. She tells me that by making her keep the baby a secret from her brothers I have cut her off from them. But she never was close to Brian and David, and Patrick always loved her. He told me while she was away with you that he missed her because he loved her more than anybody in the world, more than me or his father. Now she takes no notice of him. Granted he's two years older and not a cuddly little boy any more, but he tells her jokes and she won't laugh and he asks her riddles and she doesn't answer. I feel like shaking her.

What should I have done when she told me she was pregnant? That's what I asked her this morning. I thought we were doing the best we could in saying she was taking a year away from the university to work in a bookshop in Oxford and live with you and Terence and give a hand with your children. I know there were raised eyebrows round here when she didn't come home for Christmas but I said, 'You know what they're like at that age – they do what they feel like at the moment.' After that I began to tell people we were planning to adopt a baby due to be born in March to a girl Stella had met in Oxford. I used to have to try and get Owen to stop looking so gloomy and bowed. It aged him ten years – it really did. I'd waken in the morning seeing blue skies and then I'd remember about Stella over with you, waiting for her baby without a husband to comfort her or me to mind her, and while I was washing my face I'd cry into the wash-basin and dry away the tears with the towel because I daren't let anybody see me in that state.

I don't want to boss people about or to control their lives, but I have never found anybody else prepared to make the decisions. I've been aware of my bossiness for a long time – since just before I left school. I never told anybody at home but I decided then that I had better be a nun. I was miserable at boarding-school, homesick from morning to night, hating the way every minute was in some timetable. That's why, after me, you were made to travel to school by bike and bus, getting soaked as often as not and constantly complaining about the activities you missed. The only time I was happy was in the Chapel. You remember the Chapel – all soaring white, and our September miseries ambered by the sun through the west window while we sang the Magnificat, our voices high and pure in the very controlled plain chant? Someone told me that my red hair under the black mantilla looked beautiful in that light. I treasured the compliment. I thought if I could stay there on my knees and say, 'Here I am, Lord,' he would reach down His hand and I would reach up mine (figuratively, of course) and I could reflect His beauty and order in a pool of sunshine all the rest of my life. So I went to Sister Ambrose and told her I was thinking of becoming a nun and she said, 'Now, Kathleen, you will have to give that serious thought. We'll leave it to God's will but I myself think you are quite unsuited to community life. You must realise you have not settled happily at all during the six years you have been with us.' I told her I knew that but I was prepared to offer that up and she said, oh very drily, 'I imagine it would be an uncomfortable position for the Sisters – being offered up. The truth is, Kathleen, that you never come into any group without directing them what to do and how to do it.' I just gasped a couple of times and went out of the room.

I had never noticed it in myself but I tried to stop it and more or less managed until I got married, but, my God, Peggy, if I didn't tell everybody what to do here they would all just drift. I keep wishing they had plans of their own, for jobs or holidays or anything. I keep hoping when they don't mention anything they have secret ideas, but no. At the last minute I am asked, 'What do you think I should do?' I didn't force Stella into the university. We repeatedly asked her what she wanted to do and she shrugged or muttered that she didn't know and took herself off to her room. I thought an arts degree would be no burden to her but we didn't make her do it – it costs us plenty. We promised ourselves never to mention how little we can afford it, although sometimes nowadays Owen begins to growl about it to

Brian and David. When he catches my eye he stops. Isn't it a strange thing that she's passed every exam since then, only it doesn't seem to lift her heart at all? She sits her finals in a couple of months and then she'll be finished with study if she wants to be. There is nothing to prevent her getting a job, untrammelled, meeting people, living whatever kind of life she makes for herself. She says that by keeping Susan in the house I will never let her forget what she's been through. I don't know what to think.

Is she telling me the real truth in this version of Susan's conception or is she dressing up her weakness in the guise of decision, knowing how I laud decisiveness and deplore its lack? Or does she care what I approve of? She does hate me. She told me so and I know it to be true and I will find it difficult to live with. If the words had not been spoken I could have have coped better. If she had only glared hatred I could have told myself she was in bad form or overworked, and that anyway she is not at her best in the mornings. But she put it into words and I'll not be able to forget it. Why did I show her the letter? It was an unfriendly act, I must confess, to shake her out of her frowsty yawns. She never used to sit around like this in the mornings. Did she do it in your house? When she came home I didn't like to say anything because I thought she needed extra consideration and gentleness. While I'm dressing and feeding Susan she sits there, shows no interest, doesn't smile when Susan chuckles or chatters. She blights our enjoyment of that part of the day. She tells me now that she hates the clothes I put on Susan, trousers or dungarees and jerseys, unchanged since she herself was that age. There are frilly old-world dresses she says would suit Susan beautifully and would show she belonged to a different generation. But Susan goes out to play with all the children on the road and she would not be comfortable or indeed warm enough in pretty dresses. She is the loveliest, happiest child, Peggy, mischievous and energetic. Stella says I make a fool of myself running after her, that I am too old and too stout and that if I'm going to bend over on the footpath to lift up a struggling child I should wear tights and not stockings. Oh she can mortify me with her tongue. I felt the same shame I used to feel on the hockey field when Sister Reginald used to shout, 'Spaces, Kathleen,' and it was nothing to do with the game but with a bit of leg escaped between black stockings and navy knickers.

I hope your children never wound you, Peggy. Yours are younger, of course, but, oh dear, do be careful never to make them your enemies. You have an advantage over me in that you are affectionate and demonstrative. Why are we so different, both reared the same way? I'd like to blame the boarding-school but I can't honestly believe that I would be any more prone to hugging and kissing if I had stayed at home. Once the children are as tall as I am I no longer touch them, nor they me. I love to look at them and listen to them and think about them, but I don't touch them. Patrick will soon be out of my reach. That's why Susan is such a bonus to me.

Do you remember when I went over to bring her home? I behaved very badly and you were mad with me. I've been sorry ever since but then I could act in no other way. All I could think of was to separate Stella from the baby so that nobody would connect them in their minds, your children, your Terence, your neighbours, even though they knew, they wouldn't think in the future of the baby being anything to do with Stella if I whisked her away quickly and left Stella behind until the end of the summer. Terence wanted to show me Oxford and I wish now I had seen it properly because when will I have the chance again? All I have is a confused impression of sulphur-coloured colleges in a murky mist of rain and boated bends of river swelling quietly in fields the way no Irish river ever did. I am glad your beautiful house stands on a hill. Next time I come I will be relaxed and enjoy your company and your affluence and I won't be always on my feet with anxiety to catch the plane. Stella says I never looked at her in the hospital and it could well be true. On the plane back with the little unknown baby on my knee I thought the best thing would be for the aeroplane to fall out of the sky, through the clouds, and we'd all be dead before we hit the ground. Rather, the baby and I would be dead, never mind the other passengers, and our troubles would be over, hers and mine and Stella's too. Then I remembered Patrick at home aged eight and I hadn't even a present for him. Sure enough, when I got out of the taxi there he was on his own because Brian and David had taken themselves off hostelling in Kerry as soon as I was gone and Owen had gone to work having asked Maura next door to keep an eye on him, that he'd be all right. He burst into tears when he saw me, he was so relieved, but for ages afterwards he kept on asking me what did I need a baby for. I think he has always resented losing his place as the youngest.

Owen complained about losing his sleep with a new baby wakening up in the night and he doesn't like having the cot in our room still. There is no bedroom for Susan and he suggests putting her in with Stella. I can't do that the way things are. I used to examine Susan for resemblances to Stella. I had my answer ready for any neighbour who would see some hint. I would point out that the butcher's wife adopted two little girls who grew not only to resemble her but each other. The only family sign I could see in Susan is the way her curls grow out in circles from the crown of her head exactly the same as the white waves on my mother-in-law. But she is old and living in Kilkenny and nobody else saw it, not even Owen, but he doesn't look at Susan the way he looked at his own. There's something a bit primitive about him that he balks at bringing up another man's child. But I love her. I love her tight warm little body. I love the bright intelligent way she has of looking at me as if I always know what she has in her mind. I never enjoyed my other children. At least that's the way it seems to me, looking back. They came too close together, except Patrick, and I was tired and bothered and haunted by the death of our first baby. That knocked all the confidence out of me. I stopped being young then. Only Owen has any idea. Now I think I could bear anything in the world so long as Susan is well and happy. I waken up in the night sometimes in terror that she'd get sick or be killed in an accident and I have to get up and look at her in her cot.

If Stella is unhappy living in this house she can move out to a flat once she's in a job and Susan can have her room. Or we can build an extension when we scrape up the money. It will be for Stella to choose. I will never refer again to her outburst of this morning. That's why I'm getting it off my chest to you. I don't expect you to make any answer to all of this. Don't worry. Everything is again under control.

I will write in a day or two an ordinary letter and ask about Terence, and your children in their international school and why your children and mine and those of my neighbours have always walked on walls and shouted on Sundays while English children never do. Are we such savages? Isn't it a pity you can't relax in a holiday at home, where they could run through fields and play in barns. But our own brother having got the place has no welcome for either of us. When I have time to think of it I resent that our families are condemned to concrete, cut off by him from where we were reared. That's an exaggeration; it's probably all an exaggeration – the whole letter.

Love
Kathleen

IVY BANNISTER

My Mother's Daughter

'You're late,' my mother says sharply.

I am not. I take particular care not to be late, but I feel defensive nonetheless. My mother looks me over from head to toe. Although faded by age to a watery blue, her eyes retain their power to strike me with a sudden breathlessness, and all my inadequacies, both real and imaginary, bubble to the surface.

'That dress is too young for you, Polly,' she says. 'One of your daughters should be wearing that dress.'

My three young daughters refuse to accompany me on these visits, but I don't press the issue. Perhaps I don't like them to see me through my mother's eyes.

Her handbag waits on the bed, an exquisite relic of the forties, brocaded and elegant. With a vigour extraordinary for her years, she flings herself into her coat.

'And how is Victor?' my mother demands, not waiting for the answer, as she bustles out of her room. I trot after her, as though I were a child again. 'When people ask after me,' she says, 'tell them the truth, Polly. Explain how you've put me into a cage and thrown away the key. I don't know how you can sleep at night, knowing what you've done to me.'

It is six months now, since my mother signed herself into the nursing home, before informing her few surviving acquaintances that I'd done the dirty on her. I overheard her on the telephone, basking in the badness of her thankless daughter. 'Sharper than a serpent's tooth,' she enthused, wielding her most thrilling tones. 'What can you expect? You give up your life for them, then they dump you into the old people's home.'

My mother is a very dramatic lady. Indeed, nearly a lifetime ago, she played Juliet at the Gate Theatre.

I follow her down the green and yellow corridor towards the lift. In spite of her bad hips, her bearing is regal. The fine black cloth of her coat billows about her ankles like a coronation robe. It is impossible not to admire her. I have always admired her, and would have been glad of her admiration in return.

'I am like a caged beast in this place,' she says.

'There is nothing stopping you from moving out. They're building new flats near Seapoint.'

'Hah!' she snorts. 'Flats are for yuppies. Besides, there are not enough people about the place in a flat.' She bows her head, taking an imaginary curtain call before an imaginary audience.

The corridor smells, that tang peculiar to nursing homes of cabbage and disinfectant and urine. Sometimes at night, when I'm on my way out to a film or to a party, ready to have a good time, that smell rushes out from nowhere, burrowing up my nostrils and fogging my head. It clings to my clothes, staining the fabric of my evening with its melancholy.

The long corridor snakes around the corner, where the double windows let in a flood of light. In the recess, half-a-dozen wheelchairs are congregated, cradling the oldest and least competent inhabitants of the nursing home, a tidy row of ancient women and men, blankets tucked around them as they dribble and doze and stare.

'Just look at them,' my mother sniffs. 'Old bats! I ask you, what does a woman like me have in common with the likes of them? They are an unanswerable argument for euthanasia.'

If they hear her, in their wheelchairs, they don't react.

'Old bats!' she repeats, a shade lower, then grins, clicking her teeth.

Out the windows, you can see Bulloch Harbour and the bay. A cloud passes, its purple shadow skimming over the green sea below. I have often watched that beautiful sea from other vantage points, watched it glimmer and swirl from blue to green to grey, then back again. All of a sudden, I grab the nearest wheelchair, wheeling it around so that its aged occupant faces the water.

'Just what do you think you're doing, Polly?' my mother demands.

'Why shouldn't they look out instead of in?'

Her lips curl into a lemony smile. 'You daredevil you. If the nurse catches you, she'll eat you.'

But I swing all the wheelchairs around, just the same. 'Hurry on,' my mother says, tapping her neat foot. 'You are too sentimental for words. No doubt you'd play Beethoven to them, if you got the chance.'

*　　*　　*

My mother brushes an empty crisp packet off the passenger seat, before she sits into the car. 'I didn't let you eat crisps,' she says, 'not when you were your daughters' age. It will give them spots.'

Cautiously, I pull out into the Ulverton Road.

'Of course, I should have drowned you when you were born,' she adds reflectively. 'That's what they do with unwanted kittens.'

I am accustomed to her saying things like this. Most of the time, I try to believe that she doesn't mean them maliciously, that it's just her habitual way of communicating.

At difficult moments you need to be pleasant, my husband Victor says. So I think pleasant thoughts about home and my work and my daughters.

'I was forty-two years of age when you were born,' my mother says, 'the same age that you are now. It was a ridiculous age for calving, the single undignified episode in my entire lifetime.'

I concentrate on the road. As I turn onto the Blackrock bypass, a few substantial drops of rain splatter onto the windscreen.

'You never fetch me out of my cage on a sunny day,' my mother says. 'Yesterday the sun shone all day. You should have come yesterday.'

She snaps open her brocaded handbag, taking out a nail file. Her fingernails are still the perfect red ovals that I remember from my childhood. I used to wonder at those perfect shapes, longing to become a woman like her.

In fact, I have not turned out badly. I work in biological research, and my opinions about viruses and related creepy-crawlies are chronicled from time to time by the media.

Victor and I get on very well together, and our rearing of our children, if not exactly seamless, has so far avoided major disaster. Three peas in a pod: that's what my mother calls my daughters, reflecting unfavourably upon how they resemble their father.

The traffic crawls around Stephen's Green. My mother is growing impatient. 'I hope that you won't park too far away. Last time, I got a blister on my instep from the distance that you made me walk.'

Since the Drury Street carpark is full, I settle for the double yellow line in front of the shoe-shop, praying without conviction for mercy from the traffic wardens. I don't blame my mother for her impatience. At the age of eighty-four, I expect that I'll be impatient too.

In Bewley's she marches back through the crowd towards the plush seats under the stained-glass windows, while I queue for coffee and sticky buns. By the time that I join her, she is daubing her eyes with tissues. 'This isn't the way that it used to be,' she complains. 'There were waitresses then, and the almond buns actually tasted of almonds.'

I remember it well, my mother in her prime, whooshing past the tables in full sail, dazzling in her red cape and impossibly tall fur hat. Heads turned for her then, and the air buzzed with excited recognition. But nobody knows my mother anymore. I understand that it's not absent waitresses or inferior buns that have brought the tears to her old eyes. My heart aches, but I know better than to offer comfort. She would only brush me away.

'So,' she says brusquely, 'tell me something interesting, Polly. Impress me.'

There is no point in talking about my research, towards which she manifests a studied indifference. So I rattle on about my daughters, their enthusiasms and loathings, their flute lessons and mathematical prizes. I suspect that my mother is listening, even though her eyes sweep round and round the tea-room. She smooths her hair with a stagey gesture. The huge diamond still glitters on her hand, only her fingers have gone bony, and the loose ring has polished the skin beneath with its weight. I remember that hand, taut-skinned and plump, buttering bread, spreading jam as thickly as any child could desire. I remember those eyes, laughing and loving me. I remember loving my mother so much that the very possibility of her going away, or dying, filled me with the blackest terror. Perhaps she was really not as bad a mother as she lets on to have been.

A girl passes our table in a flapping dress, unbuttoned from hem to crotch, exposing lavender tights and heavy black shoes. 'And she thinks she looks gorgeous,' my mother sniffs. 'You used to do things like that to me, Polly. You shamed me with your vulgar clothing. Not to mention those misfits that you fell in love with. I'll never forget that dreadful what's-his-name from Crumlin, the one whose eyes moved in opposite directions.'

I smile brightly at my mother, pretending that I feel no pain, but I'm glad that our coffee's drunk and it's time to go.

She is quiet for most of the journey back, melted into the passenger seat, every muscle relaxed. It is the way she often behaves, as if reserving her energies for her next performance. Suddenly, she pulls herself upright. 'What I resent the most about you, Polly,' she says softly, 'is how happily you married. Your father was such a peasant. He never had what I wanted, not when I wanted it.'

Cautiously, I glance at her. It's a possibility I've never considered before: that she might be envious. She glints at me with a seabird's eye, about to devour a sprat. Then I remember a day trip, twenty years in the past, when she tried to cajole Victor, then my fiancé, into marrying another girl. I shiver once again at this treachery.

'When I was growing up, we had a maid named Polly,' my mother hisses. 'She was an ignorant Welsh girl. I named you after her.'

I can't take anymore. I pull the wheel hard, turning the corner into the nursing home drive so fast that the gravel spits under my tyres. I speed recklessly through the narrow stone archway into the carpark. I jump out. The passenger door creaks open. I am counting the seconds now.

We drag through reception into the lift. My mother has begun to smile. She looks younger than her eighty-four years, and somehow radiant. I follow her into her room. 'I'm feeling quite refreshed now,' she says. 'You'd be surprised how I look forward to our little encounters.'

My chest is tight. My head is thumping. I brush my lips against her stiff cheek. Not bothering with the lift I flee down the stairs, out, out into the sea air. I barely make it to the car before the tears come, cascading down my cheeks. With shaking hands, I light the single cigarette of my week; I smoke, gasping through my tears.

Then I square my shoulders and become myself again, Polly

McKenna, the capable woman created by my failed efforts to dazzle my mother, the woman that other people know and respect. And once again, I am no longer my mother's daughter. At least not for another week.

EDNA O'BRIEN

Cords

Everything was ready, the suitcase closed, her black velvet coat-collar carefully brushed, and a list pinned to the wall reminding her husband when to feed the hens and turkeys, and what foodstuffs to give them. She was setting out on a visit to her daughter Claire in London, just like any mother, except that her daughter was different: she'd lost her faith, and she mixed with queer people and wrote poems. If it was stories one could detect the sin in them, but these poems made no sense at all and therefore seemed more wicked. Her daughter had sent the money for the air-ticket. She was going now, kissing her husband good-bye, tender towards him in a way that she never was, throughout each day, as he spent his time looking through the window at the wet currant bushes, grumbling about the rain, but was in fact pleased at the excuse to hatch indoors, and asked for tea all the time, which he lapped from a saucer, because it was more pleasurable.

'The turkeys are the most important,' she said, kissing him good-bye, and thinking faraway to the following Christmas, to the turkeys she would sell, and the plumper ones she would give as gifts.

'I hope you have a safe flight,' he said. She'd never flown before.

'All Irish planes are blessed, they never crash,' she said, believing totally in the God that created her, sent her this venial husband, a largish farmhouse, hens, hardship, and one daughter who'd changed, become moody, and grown away from them completely.

The journey was pleasant once she'd got over the shock of being strapped down for the take-off. As they went higher and higher she looked out at the very white, waspish cloud and thought of the wash tub and hoped her husband would remember to change his shirt while she was away. The trip would have been perfect but that there was a screaming woman who had to be calmed down by the air hostess. She looked like a woman who was being sent to a mental institution, but did not know it.

Claire met her mother at the airport and they kissed warmly, not having seen each other for over a year.

'Have you stones in it?' Claire said, taking the fibre suitcase. It was doubly secured with a new piece of binding twine. Her mother wore a black straw hat with clusters of cherries on both sides of the brim.

'You were great to meet me,' the mother said.

'Of course I'd meet you,' Claire said, easing her mother right back on the taxi seat. It was a long ride and they might as well be comfortable.

'I could have navigated,' the mother said, and Claire said

nonsense a little too brusquely. Then to make amends she asked gently how the journey was.

'Oh I must tell you, there was this very peculiar woman and she was screaming.'

Claire listened and stiffened, remembering her mother's voice that became low and dramatic in a crisis, the same voice that said, 'Sweet Lord your father will kill us', or, 'What's to become of us, the bailiff is here', or, 'Look, look, the chimney is on fire.'

'But otherwise?' Claire said. This was a holiday, not an expedition into the past.

'We had tea and sandwiches. I couldn't eat mine, the bread was buttered.'

'Still faddy?' Claire said. Her mother got bilious if she touched butter, fish, olive oil, or eggs; although her daily diet was mutton stew, or home-cured bacon.

'Anyhow, I have nice things for you,' Claire said. She had bought in stocks of biscuits, jellies and preserves because these were the things her mother favoured, these foods that she herself found distasteful.

The first evening passed well enough. The mother unpacked the presents – a chicken, bread, eggs, a tapestry of a church spire which she'd done all winter, stitching at it until she was almost blind, a holy water font, ashtrays made from shells, lamps converted from bottles, and a picture of a matador assembled by sticking small varnished pebbles on to hardboard.

Claire laid them along the mantelshelf in the kitchen, and stood back, not so much to admire them as to see how incongruous they looked, piled together.

'Thank you,' she said to her mother, as tenderly as she

might have when she was a child. These gifts touched her, especially the tapestry, although it was ugly. She thought of the winter nights and the Aladdin lamp smoking (they expected the electricity to be installed soon), and her mother hunched over her work, not even using a thimble to ease the needle through, because she believed in sacrifice, and her father turning to say, 'Could I borrow your glasses, Mam, I want to have a look at the paper?' He was too lazy to have his own eyes tested and believed that his wife's glasses were just as good. She could picture them at the fire night after night, the turf flames green and fitful, the hens locked up, foxes prowling around in the wind, outside.

'I'm glad you like it, I did it specially for you,' the mother said gravely, and they both stood with tears in their eyes, savouring those seconds of tenderness, knowing that it would be short-lived.

'You'll stay seventeen days,' Claire said, because that was the length an economy ticket allowed. She really meant, 'Are you staying seventeen days?'

'If it's all right,' her mother said over-humbly. 'I don't see you that often, and I miss you.'

Claire withdrew into the scullery to put on the kettle for her mother's hot water bottle; she did not want any disclosures now, any declaration about how hard life had been and how near they'd been to death during many of the father's drinking deliriums.

'Your father sent you his love,' her mother said, nettled because Claire had not asked how he was.

'How is he?'

'He's great now, never touches a drop.'

Claire knew that if he had, he would have descended on

her, the way he used to descend on her as a child when she was in the convent, or else she would have had a telegram, of clipped urgency, 'Come home. Mother.'

'It was God did it, curing him like that,' the mother said.

Claire thought bitterly that God had taken too long to help the thin frustrated man who was emaciated, crazed and bankrupted by drink. But she said nothing, she merely filled the rubber bottle, pressed the air from it with her arm, and then conducted her mother upstairs to bed.

Next morning they went up to the centre of London and Claire presented her mother with fifty pounds. The woman got flushed and began to shake her head, the quick uncontrolled movements resembling those of a beast with the staggers.

'You always had a good heart, too good,' she said to her daughter, as her eyes beheld racks of coats, raincoats, skirts on spinning hangers, and all kinds and colours of hats.

'Try some on,' Claire said. 'I have to make a phone call.'

There were guests due to visit her that night – it had been arranged weeks before – but as they were bohemian people, she could not see her mother suffering them, or them suffering her mother. There was the added complication that they were a 'trio' – one man and two women; his wife and his mistress. At that point in their lives the wife was noticeably pregnant.

On the telephone the mistress said they were looking forward, awfully, to the night, and Claire heard herself substantiate the invitation by saying she had simply rung up to remind them. She thought of asking another man to give a complexion of decency to the evening, but the only three unattached men she could think of had been lovers of hers and she could not call on them; it seemed pathetic.

'Damn,' she said, irritated by many things, but mainly by

the fact that she was going through one of those bleak, loveless patches that come in everyone's life, but, she imagined, came more frequently the older one got. She was twenty-eight. Soon she would be thirty. Withering.

'How do?' her mother said in a ridiculous voice when Claire returned. She was holding a hand mirror up to get a back view of a ridiculous hat, which she had tried on. It resembled the shiny straw she wore for her trip, except that it was more ornamental and cost ten guineas. That was the second point about it that Claire noted. The white price tag was hanging over the mother's nose. Claire hated shopping the way other people might hate going to the dentist. For herself she never shopped. She merely saw things in windows, ascertained the size, and bought them.

'Am I too old for it?' the mother said. A loaded question in itself.

'You're not,' Claire said. 'You look well in it.'

'Of course I've always loved hats,' her mother said, as if admitting to some secret vice. Claire remembered drawers with felt hats laid into them, and bobbins on the brims of hats, and little aprons of veiling, with spots which, as a child, she thought might crawl over the wearer's face.

'Yes, I remember your hats,' Claire said, remembering too the smell of empty perfume bottles and camphor, and a saxe-blue hat that her mother once got on approbation, by post, and wore to Mass before returning it to the shop.

'If you like it, take it,' Claire said indulgently.

The mother bought it, along with a reversible rain-coat and a pair of shoes. She told the assistant who measured her feet about a pair of shoes which lasted her for seventeen years, and were eventually stolen by a tinker-woman, who afterwards was sent to jail for the theft.

'Poor old creature I wouldn't have wished jail on her,' the mother said, and Claire nudged her to shut up. The mother's face flushed under the shelter of her new, wide-brimmed hat.

'Did I say something wrong?' she said as she descended uneasily on the escalator, her parcels held close to her.

'No, I just thought she was busy, it isn't like shops at home,' Claire said.

'I think she was enjoying the story,' her mother said, gathering courage before she stepped off, on to the ground floor.

At home they prepared the food and the mother tidied the front room before the visitors arrived. Without a word she carried all her own trophies – the tapestry, the pebble picture, the ashtrays, the holy water font and the other ornaments – and put them in the front room alongside the books, the pencil drawings and the poster of Bengal that was a left-over from Claire's dark-skinned lover.

'They're nicer in here,' the mother said, apologizing for doing it, and at the same time criticising the drawing of the nude.

'I'd get rid of some of those things if I were you,' she said in a serious tone to her daughter.

Claire kept silent, and sipped the whisky she felt she needed badly. Then to get off the subject she asked after her mother's feet. They were fixing a chiropodist appointment for the next day.

The mother had changed into a blue blouse, Claire into velvet pants, and they sat before the fire on low pouffes with a blue-shaded lamp casting a restful light on their very similar faces. At sixty, and made-up, the mother still had a poem of a face: round, pale, perfect and with soft eyes, expectant, in spite of what life had brought. On the whites there had appeared blobs of green, the sad green of old age.

'You have a tea-leaf on your eyelid,' she said to Claire, putting up her hand to brush it away. It was mascara which got so smeared that Claire had to go upstairs to repair it.

At that precise moment the visitors came.

'They're here,' the mother said when the hall bell shrieked.

'Open the door,' Claire called down.

'Won't it look odd, if you don't do it?' the mother said.

'Oh, open it,' Claire called impatiently. She was quite relieved that they would have to muddle through their own set of introductions.

The dinner went off well. They all liked the food and the mother was not as shy as Claire expected. She told about her journey, but kept the 'mad woman' episode out of it, and about a television programme she'd once seen, showing how bird's nest soup was collected. Only her voice was unnatural.

After dinner Claire gave her guests enormous brandies, because she felt relieved that nothing disastrous had been uttered. Her mother never drank spirits of course.

The fulfilled guests sat back, sniffed brandy, drank their coffee, laughed, tipped their cigarette ash on the floor, having missed the ashtray by a hair's breadth, gossiped, and re-filled their glasses. They smiled at the various new ornaments but did not comment, except to say that the tapestry was nice.

'Claire likes it,' the mother said timidly, drawing them

131

into another silence. The evening was punctuated by brief but crushing silences.

'You like Chinese food then?' the husband said. He mentioned a restaurant which she ought to go and see. It was in the East End of London and getting there entailed having a motor-car.

'You've been there?' his wife said to the young blonde mistress who had hardly spoken.

'Yes and it was super except for the pork which was drowned in Chanel Number Five. Remember?' she said, turning to the husband, who nodded.

'We must go some time,' his wife said. 'If ever you can spare an evening.' She was staring at the big brandy snifter that she let rock back and forth in her lap. It was for rose petals but when she saw it she insisted on drinking from it. The petals were already dying on the mantelshelf.

'That was the night we found a man against a wall, beaten up,' the mistress said, shivering, recalling how she had actually shivered.

'You were so sorry for him,' the husband said, amused.

'Wouldn't anyone be?' the wife said tartly, and Claire turned to her mother and promised that they would go to that restaurant the following evening.

'We'll see,' the mother said. She knew the places she wanted to visit: Buckingham Palace, the Tower of London and the waxworks museum. When she went home it was these places she would discuss with her neighbours who'd already been to London, not some seamy place where men were flung against walls.

'No, not another, it's not good for the baby,' the husband

said, as his wife balanced her empty glass on the palm of her hand and looked towards the bottle.

'Who's the more important, me or the baby?'

'Don't be silly, Marigold,' the husband said.

'Excuse me,' she said in a changed voice. 'Whose welfare are you thinking about?' She was on the verge of an emotional outburst, her cheeks flushed from brandy and umbrage. By contrast Claire's mother had the appearance of a tombstone, chalk white and deadly still.

'How is the fire?' Claire said, staring at it. On that cue her mother jumped up and sailed off with the coal scuttle.

'I'll get it,' Claire said following. The mother did not even wait until they reached the kitchen.

'Tell me,' she said, her blue eyes pierced with insult, 'which of those two ladies is he married to?'

'It's not your concern,' Claire said, hastily. She had meant to smooth it over, to say that the pregnant woman had some mental disturbance, but instead she said hurtful things about her mother being narrow-minded and cruel.

'Show me your friends and I know who you are,' the mother said and went away to shovel the coal. She left the filled bucket outside the living-room door and went upstairs. Claire, who had gone back to her guests, heard the mother's footsteps climbing the stairs and going into the bedroom overhead.

'Is your mother gone to bed?' the husband asked.

'She's tired I expect,' Claire said, conveying weariness too. She wanted them to go. She could not confide in them even though they were old friends. They might sneer. They were not friends any more than the ex-lovers, they were all social appendages, extras, acquaintances cultivated in order to be able to say to other acquaintances, 'Well one night a bunch of us went mad and had a nude sit-in . . .' There was no one she trusted, no one she could produce for her mother and feel happy about it.

'Music, brandy, cigarettes . . .' They were recalling her, voicing their needs, wondering who would go to the machine for the cigarettes. Pauline did. They stayed until they'd finished the packet, which was well after midnight.

Claire hurried to her mother's room and found her awake with the light on, fingering her horn rosary beads. The same old black ones.

'I'm sorry,' Claire said.

'You turned on me like a tinker,' her mother said, in a voice cracked with emotion.

'I didn't mean to,' Claire said. She tried to sound reasonable, assured; she tried to tell her mother that the world was a big place and contained many people, all of whom held various views about various things.

'They're not sincere,' her mother said, stressing the last word.

'And who is?' Claire said, remembering the treacherous way the lovers vanished, or how former landladies rigged meters so that units of electricity cost double. Her mother had no notion of how lonely it was to read manuscripts all day, and write a poem once in a while, when one became consumed with a memory or an idea, and then to constantly go out, seeking people, hoping that one of them might fit, might know the shorthand of her, body and soul.

'I was a good mother, I did everything I could, and this is all the thanks I get.' It was spoken with such justification that Claire turned and laughed, hysterically. An incident leaped to her tongue, something she had never recalled before.

'You went to hospital,' she said to her mother, 'to have your toe lanced, and you came home and told me, me, that the doctor said, "Raise your right arm until I give you an injection", but when you did, he gave you no injection, he just cut into your toe. Why did you tell it?' The words fell out of her mouth unexpectedly, and she became aware of the awfulness when she felt her knees shaking.

'What are you talking about?' her mother said numbly. The face that was round, in the evening, had become old, twisted, bitter.

'Nothing,' Claire said. Impossible to explain. She had violated all the rules: decency, kindness, caution. She would never be able to laugh it off in the morning. Muttering an apology she went to her own room and sat on her bed, trembling. Since her mother's arrival every detail of her childhood kept dogging her. Her present life, her work, the friends she had, seemed insubstantial compared with all that had happened before. She could count the various batches of white, hissing geese – it was geese in those days – that wandered over the swampy fields, one year after another, hid in memory she could locate the pot-holes on the driveway where rain lodged, and where leaking oil from a passing car made rainbows. Looking down into rainbows to escape the colour that was in her mind, or on her tongue. She'd licked four fingers once that were slit by an unexpected razor blade which was wedged upright in a shelf where she'd reached to find a sweet, or to finger the secret dust up there. The same colour had been on her mother's violated toe underneath the big, bulky bandage. In chapel too, the sanctuary light was a bowl of blood with a flame laid into it. These images did not distress her at the time. She used to love to slip into the chapel, alone, in the daytime, moving from one Station of the Cross to the next, being God's exclusive pet, praying that she would die before her mother did, in order to escape being the scapegoat of her father. How could she have known, how could any of them have known that twenty years later, zipped into a heated, plastic tent, treating herself to a steam bath she would suddenly panic and cry out convinced that her sweat became as drops of blood. She put her hands through the flaps and begged the masseuse to protect her, the way she had begged her mother, long ago. Made a fool of herself. The way she made a fool of herself with the various men. The first night she met the Indian she was wearing a white fox collar, and its whiteness under his dark, well-chiselled chin made a stark sight as they walked through a mirrored room to a table, and saw, and were seen in mirrors. He said something she couldn't hear.

'Tell me later,' she said, already putting her little claim on him, already saying. 'You are not going to abandon me in this room of mirrors, in my bluish-white fox that so compliments your bluish-black lips.' But after a few weeks he left, like the others. She was familiar with the various tactics of withdrawal – abrupt, honest, nice. Flowers, notes posted from the provinces, and the 'I don't want you to get hurt' refrain. They reminded her of the trails that slugs leave on a lawn in summer mornings, the sad, silver trails of departure. Their goings were far more vivid than their comings, or was she only capable of remembering the worst? Remembering everything, solving nothing. She undressed, she told herself that her four fingers had healed, that her mother's big toe was now like any other person's big toe, that her father drank tea and held his temper, and that one day she would meet a man whom she loved and did not frighten away. But it was brandy optimism. She'd gone down and carried the bottle up. The brandy gave her hope but it disturbed her heart beats and she was unable to sleep. As morning approached she rehearsed the sweet and conciliatory things she would say to her mother.

They went to Mass on Sunday, but it was obvious that Claire was not in the habit of going: they had to ask the way. Going in, her mother took a small liqueur bottle from her handbag and filled it with holy water from the font.

'It's always good to have it,' she said to Claire, but in a bashful way. The outburst had severed them, and they were polite now in a way that should never have been.

After Mass they went – because the mother had stated her wishes – to the waxworks museum, saw the Tower of London and walked across the park that faced Buckingham Palace.

'Very good grazing here,' the mother said. Her new shoes were getting spotted from the damp, highish grass. It was raining. The spokes of the mother's umbrella kept tapping Claire's, and no matter how far she drew away, the mother moved accordingly, to prong her, it seemed.

'You know,' the mother said. 'I was thinking.'

Claire knew what was coming. Her mother wanted to go home; she was worried about her husband, her fowls, the washing that would have piled up, the spring wheat that would have to be sown. In reality she was miserable. She and her daughter were farther away now than when they wrote letters each week and discussed the weather, or work, or the colds they'd had.

'You're only here six days,' Claire said, 'And I want to take you to the theatre and restaurants. Don't go.'

'I'll think about it,' the mother said. But her mind was made up.

Two evenings later they waited in the airport lounge, hesitant to speak, for fear they might miss the flight number.

'The change did you good,' Claire said. Her mother was togged out in new clothes and looked smarter. She had two more new hats in her hand, carrying them in the hope they would escape the notice of the customs men.

'I'll let you know if I have to pay duty on them,' she said.

'Do,' Claire said, smiling, straightening her mother's collar, wanting to say something endearing, something that would atone, without having to go over their differences, word for word.

'No one can say but that you fitted me out well, look at all my style,' the mother said smiling at her image in the glass door of the telephone box. 'And our trip up the river,' she said. 'I think I enjoyed it more than anything.' She was referring to a short trip they'd taken down the Thames to Westminster. They had planned to go in the opposite direction towards the greenness of Kew and Hampton Court but they'd left it – at least Claire had left it – too late and could only go towards the city on a passenger boat that was returning from those green places.

Claire had been miserly with her time and on that particular evening she'd sat at her desk pretending to work, postponing the time until she got up and rejoined her mother, who was downstairs sewing on all the buttons that had fallen off over the years. And now the mother was thanking her, saying it had been lovely. Lovely. They had passed warehouses and cranes brought to their evening standstill yellow and tilted, pylons like floodlit honeycombs in the sky, and boats, and gasworks, and filthy chimneys. The spring evening had been drenched with sewerage smell and yet her mother went on being thankful.

'I hope my mad lady won't be aboard,' the mother said, trying to make a joke out of it now.

'Not likely,' Claire said, but the mother declared that life was full of strange and sad coincidences. They looked at each other, looked away, criticised a man who was wolfing sandwiches from his pocket, looked at the airport clock and compared the time on their watches.

'Sssh . . . sssh . . .' Claire had to say.

'That's it,' they both said then, relieved. As if they had secretly feared the flight number would never be called.

At the barrier they kissed, their damp cheeks touched and stayed for a second like that, each registering the other's sorrow.

'I'll write to you, I'll write oftener,' Claire said, and for a few minutes she stood there waving, weeping, not aware that the visit was over and that she could go back to her own life now, such as it was.

MARY LAVIN

Senility

A da was steeping her sheets when her daughter surprised her by arriving on her doorstep.

'What on earth are you doing, Mummy?' Laura cried. 'I thought you sent heavy things to the laundry.'

Ada saw no reason to explain that she'd had an accident during the night. 'I didn't hear the car,' she said. 'Did you honk the horn?'

'Of course,' Ada murmured apologetically. Laura had good reason to be abrupt. She never went by without honking in case Ada needed something from the shops, but Ada, priding herself on never running short mid-week, always ran to the window and signalled that she needed nothing. Laura looked again at the wet sheets. Somehow she guessed what had happened. 'Oh, Mummy, I don't believe it! You must be getting senile,' she said with a laugh. Left to herself Ada would not have seen anything remotely funny about the mishap, but she laughed too.

Laura rolled up her sleeves. 'Here, let me wring them out for you,' she said.

'Not at all.' Ada gave her a little push. 'Off you go! I know you have a lot to do.' She went to the door with her. 'I'll be seeing you tonight, I expect?'

'Yes. Me or John,' Laura said. Then from the gate she called back. 'Next week, when you're under the same roof with us, you'll be able to call me during the night whenever anything like this happens.'

'It's hardly going to be a nightly occurrence,' Ada said.

'I didn't mean that,' Laura said and chastened, she got into her car, waved, and drove away.

Ada was a bit rattled by the visit. For one thing, Laura ought to know how she felt about the word senile. It was a word that had for a long time been a source of friction between them, dating from the death of Ada's own mother, who, in her late eighties, had had to be put into a home for the aged because of physical debility. For some reason Laura liked to say the old woman had been mentally disturbed at the end, but apart from their disagreement on this, Laura and Ada got on famously. Ada had no real misgivings about selling her house and going to live with her daughter. Now, rinsing out the sheets, she wrung them again and went out to spread them on the grass.

It was a beautiful day and the garden was at its best. Ada had a momentary pang at the thought of leaving, but the house really was too large for one person living alone. It was only common sense to 'join forces' with the young couple, as John put it so generously, considering she wouldn't be contributing to the household. The young people had no need of money from her. They knew of course that one day all she possessed would belong to them.

A week later, on the day after the sale, John took another morning off to move Ada and her personal belongings. They had arranged to stop off at the bank to lodge the proceeds of the sale, and after they had made the lodgement Ada took the occasion to be explicit about the terms of her will. Then on a sudden impulse she sounded a cautionary note.

'Let's hope there won't be any unexpected demands on my money. I dread the thought that my small resources could be drained away in some tiresome illness.'

'There'll be no fear of that,' John said firmly. 'Laura intends to keep you wrapped up in cotton wool!'

'Thank you, John.' Ada was grateful. 'You realise of course that I like to feel that when I die I'll be leaving you and Laura some token of my love and gratitude.'

'We appreciate that, Ada.' John squeezed her arm. He was more gracious than Laura, who took no interest whatever in this subject. Later that very morning, after John had left Ada off and gone back to the office, Laura was almost rude when Ada attempted to show her pass-book.

'By the time you die, Mummy, your nest-egg will seem very small to John and me – well, relatively small anyway!' And seeing that Ada was hurt by this, she became downright impatient. 'You ought to be glad we don't need any money from you,' she said. The two women were up in the room that was to be Ada's, a very nice room. 'Take my advice, Mummy, and spend your money on yourself.' Leaning over, she gave Ada a very sweet kiss. 'It's time you had it easy,' she said, so lovingly that Ada would have been extraordinarily happy, if the next moment Laura had not spoiled everything.

'Keep well and look after yourself, Mummy. You wouldn't want to be a burden on everyone like poor Grandmother, would you?'

'Your grandmother was never a great burden on me, Laura,' Ada said. 'If I had had more fortitude, I could have kept her at home with us till the end, and not put her into that dreadful place.' She sighed. 'I see that now, when it's too late.'

'Rubbish.' Laura pursed her lips. 'Not after she got —'

'Please! Don't say that word, I beg of you. Not today of all days.'

'What do you mean by that?' Laura stopped gathering up the empty cartons that had contained the few possessions Ada had kept.

'You wouldn't understand,' Ada said. Mercifully, Laura did not press the point any further.

By mid-day the room was as neat and tidy as when it was the spare room, ready at a moment's notice to house an overnight guest.

'I hope you'll be comfortable here, Mummy.' Laura looked around the room. 'If you like, John can move your armchair to face the window. We put it there so you'd have your back to the light for reading, or for taking your nap in the afternoon.'

'But I never take a nap,' Ada protested.

'Oh, I forgot,' Laura said lightly. She went over to the bed and lifted the chintz valance to expose the mattress. 'You ought to sleep well at night, anyway. We got a new mattress.'

Ada felt that this was an unnecessary extravagance, but she didn't say so. Instead she followed Laura downstairs. It was time for lunch.

'Now! How are we going to spend the rest of the day?' Laura asked, when they got up from the table.

'You must attend to your own affairs, dear,' Ada said. 'You've lost a lot of time on me, already.'

'Oh, that's all right, I decided to devote the whole day to you.'

'Ah well, in that case,' Ada said happily, 'why don't we go out in the garden?' She was thinking of the two big boxes of plants and rooted cuttings she'd dug up in her own garden before the sale, and which were in the garage waiting to be planted.

But Laura shivered.

'It's far too cold.'

'Not for me,' Ada said.

'Ah well, I was never as hardy as you, Mummy. But I suppose those plants you brought ought to be put into the ground soon?'

'The sooner the better,' Ada said, 'but, if you like, they could be heeled-in in some sheltered corner, and left till next spring.'

'Oh, could they?' Laura seemed relieved. Then she thought of all the room they were taking up, and she frowned again. 'That would be just as much work as planting them properly.' She glanced out of the window. 'Let's leave them where they are for the moment, anyway.'

The day passed pleasantly for Ada, and that evening, after a very good dinner, she went up to bed deliberately early to give the young people some time to themselves. It was nice to hear the murmur of their voices below as she was dropping off to sleep.

She was, therefore, absolutely mortified to wake in the small hours of that night and find she had had another accident. She sprang out of bed to see what damage she had done. Luckily the mattress had come through safe. She pulled off the bottom sheet and threw it on the floor. Then, stumbling out of her room, she crossed the landing to the linen room, got out a clean sheet and made up the bed again. Once back in bed, she briefly regretted that she hadn't taken Laura up on her offer to bring her breakfast in bed, but she'd felt that the least she could do was to make an appearance before John left the house for the office.

The next morning, Ada ran into Laura on the landing as Laura was hurrying down herself, and although Ada was reluctant to make the disclosure, she did so in a quick whisper.

'The mattress is unharmed though,' she added.

'Oh, bother the mattress!' Laura said. 'It's you I'm concerned about. Why didn't you call me? I could have got you clean sheets.'

'I didn't want to wake you, so I helped myself.'

'Oh?' Laura seemed surprised. 'Where did you find the sheets?'

'In the linen room, of course.'

'I meant on what shelf?' Laura said. 'I try to rotate the linen.'

'I see.' Ada understood, but next minute Laura looked anxiously at her.

'I wonder what's causing this to happen?' she said.

'I'm afraid it's like losing a tooth, or getting one's first grey hair,' Ada said. 'It's an intimation of mortality.'

Laura had to laugh. 'Mummy, you're quite a wag. I must tell that to John,' she said.

'Laura! It would be most indelicate to mention this to your husband.'

'Oh dear. I suppose it could be embarrassing for you.

I won't say a word.' Together they went down to the breakfast room.

John had finished, and was wiping his mouth with his napkin. He put the napkin down, stood up and pulled out Ada's chair, but when Ada turned to thank him, he was gone.

'He'll be back!' Laura said, and she winked. 'He's as fastidious as a cat about these early-morning matters.'

Ada ate her first really hearty breakfast in years. She felt in fine fettle, and when John came back into the breakfast room, with his coat on, and carrying his hat and briefcase, he gave both women a peck on the cheek. When he was finally gone for good, Laura turned around.

'Well, what are you going to do with yourself today, Mummy?' she asked. 'It's a glorious day! Perhaps we ought to put in those plants you brought?'

'I could put them in alone,' Ada said, but Laura wouldn't hear of it.

'I don't get nearly enough fresh air,' she said. She did look pale, Ada thought, but again she forbore from saying what she thought. She hoped her own zeal for gardening might become contagious. And indeed, all that week, Laura did spend a lot of time out of doors with her. The days flew. Even when Laura wasn't with her, the time went fast because there was so much to do. The garden was not neglected, but Laura and John had no feeling for plants and no interest whatever in texture or tone, or the need for contrasting effects. Ada worked like a trooper, but she took care not to make any large-scale alterations, although when, on occasion, she did nervously make a change, Laura and John neither noticed nor cared. Day by day, Ada became happier.

Then, about six months after she'd moved in with them,

Ada had another mishap. This time she was devastated. Again she sprang out of bed in an agony of concern for the bedding, but there was no real harm done. Once again she pulled off the wet sheet, and once again she staggered out to the linen closet, wishing she'd asked Laura to explain her system of rotation. But the door of the linen room was locked! Ada had no recourse but to go back to her room and make the best of things, wrapping herself up in a cocoon of blankets. When she woke again it was morning, and the house was stirring into life. Scrambling into her clothes, she threw the coverlet over the bed and left the room. On the stairs, she met her daughter, who was running back up to get a clean handkerchief for her husband. Ada didn't stop to tell her about the incident. Yet she had barely taken her place at the table, and said good morning to John, when Laura stormed back into the breakfast room.

'Not again, Mummy! What on earth is the matter?'

Ada gave Laura a stony look and turned to her son-in-law, but he was slipping away from the table. Her only option was to face her daughter.

'What brought you into my room anyway?' she asked. 'I thought you were running up to get a clean handkerchief for your husband?' Laura pointed to where, beside her plate, a neatly folded handkerchief waited, presumably to be given in exchange for a soiled, and no doubt disgusting, one which John would produce and hand over to her on returning to the room. Not across the table, Ada prayed. Not across the food! Then her mind returned to her problem. 'There's no need for you to interfere,' she said. 'I can attend to the matter myself. I would have done so already, only the door of the linen room was locked. Against whom, may I ask?'

147

'Oh, don't be so touchy,' Laura said.

Ada heard her son-in-law's footsteps approaching.

'Let's drop the subject,' she said.

John came into the room all smiles.

'Good-bye, girls. Have a good day.'

After they heard his car drive away, the two women were somewhat constrained.

'Is there more coffee in that thing?' Ada asked at last, deliberately disparaging the pretty little porcelain coffee-pot, the daily use of which she secretly respected.

Laura poured her another cup. 'Is that hot? I could make more.'

'No. This is all right.' Ada was not to be blandished. 'You didn't tell me why you went into my room? I know this is your house, but surely I'm allowed the privacy of my bedroom?'

'Oh, Mummy. Don't be mean! I was worried about you.'

'Nonsense,' Ada said.

'But this is happening so *often*.'

'I'd like to know what you consider often?' Ada said hotly, and this, she was glad to see, broke down Laura's reserves.

'Oh, Mummy, darling,' the girl cried. 'I couldn't bear it if anything happened to you. It would break my heart.'

Ada looked away.

'Anyone would think the world was coming to an end,' she said. She stood up. 'What about that sheet? Give it to me.'

'I'll get it,' Laura said humbly. 'And I'll help you make the bed.' She glanced out of the window. It was another glorious day. 'Let's go out in the garden. Do you remember when we were putting in those pinks, you said that after they took root we could take slips from them – slips or cuttings or whatever it is they're called.'

It pleased Ada beyond measure to have Laura defer to her gardening skill, but she did not jump at the suggestion. 'Let's attend to the bed first,' she said in a practical fashion.

When the bed was made and they had tidied up the room, Laura took the crumpled sheet and dumped it in the laundry bin.

'Shouldn't we rinse it?' Ada asked.

Laura shrugged her shoulders.

'Why bother! Let's wash the breakfast dishes and then go out in the sun and enjoy ourselves.'

It was Laura, though, who was unable to forget.

'Are you sure you're all right, Mummy?' she asked, not once but twice, while they were washing up the breakfast things. In the end Ada found her own mind straying back to the indignity of the night.

'Oh, Laura,' she cried out of her thoughts. 'How I hate to think of the humiliation your grandmother must have suffered at the hands of those nurses. They were wholly lacking in delicacy.'

'It's too late to worry about it now,' Laura said easily. 'Grandmother was too far gone for niceties, anyway.'

'On the contrary!' Ada said sharply. 'She was too quick by half! Do you know, it's my belief, Laura, that deep down she regarded that place as a kind of workhouse, and I think she cherished a secret grudge against me for putting her there.'

'If that's the case, then she was a fool,' Laura said bluntly. 'And you're a worse fool to let it bother you, particularly when she was –'

'Laura! *Please!* Your grandmother was sharp and bright in

her mind up to the very end. Let me tell you something that happened in that place not long before she died.' The incident Ada had in mind suddenly brought tears to her eyes. 'The poor little thing,' she said.

'For heaven's sake, Mummy! I thought you'd come to terms with yourself about all that business.'

'No, dear. No.' Ada said. 'I mean, yes. Yes,' she said hastily, correcting herself. 'I have come to terms with myself, but what I'm going to tell you underlines the limitations of those geriatric units. You see, when I went to visit your grandmother, I used to creep into the ward on tiptoe in case the other old women were dozing, as they usually were, but one day when I'd crept in, what do you think I found? Bedlam! Standing beside your grandmother's bed, one on either side, were two young nurses laughing their heads off. Not nice laughing either. Ugly, vulgar laughing.'

'What were they laughing at?'

'That's what I wanted to know,' Ada said. 'They were behaving like ward-maids. They'd just taken up your grandmother's newspaper – you remember of course that I used to have the daily paper sent in to her? She always liked to glance at it, although towards the end I used to find it wrapped at the foot of her bed, because nobody had bothered to unwrap it. If anyone had gone to the trouble of unrolling it and flattening it out, I'm sure she would have shown some interest in it.' Here, however, Ada stopped short. 'Laura! I hope you read the daily paper, or at least run your eye over the editorials, because –' Ada stopped again. 'What was I saying, dear?'

'Something about two ward-maids?'

'No, Laura, no. They weren't ward-maids, they were trained

nurses. Trained indeed! I'm afraid their training left a lot to be desired. Nowhere on earth is as noisy as a hospital, and it is the nurses that make all the noise, banging things about and talking at the top of their voices. As for those trolleys they wheel around at meal-times, laden with metal trays! Why metal? Tell me that! Your grandmother used to wince with pain – actual pain – at that sound. But that was nothing to what some of the other patients had to suffer. I remember particularly those poor bloated women in the other beds – obese, that's the medical word for them, although gross would be my word. But, anyway, God help them, did you know that when the nurses were making their beds, or had to turn them over to change a dressing, they used to call in the porter to lift them? Think of that for humiliation. Your grandmother was not heavy. On the contrary, she was too slight, too fragile – which, by the way, was probably why she never, as far as I know, suffered from bed sores – but her bones were brittle, breakable as glass I was told. When they went to give her a bath, they still had to get the porter to lift her in and out of the tub. When she told me this I tried to pretend to her they were male nurses, but I know she didn't believe me. Laura! Are you listening?'

'Yes, of course,' Laura said, 'but get on with it, Mummy! What were the silly bitches doing?'

'Bitches. Oh, you mean the nurses. It was what they were saying I minded – that, and their ugly sniggering. They had your grandmother pitifully perplexed. And as you know Laura, where the aged are concerned, perplexity can be a severe mental anguish which –'

'Never mind the theorising, Mummy. Get on with the story.'

Ada hastened to comply. 'Those dreadful women had for once opened your grandmother's newspaper, but they were holding it up in front of her and quizzing her about a picture on the front page. *"Who is that? I suppose you know him too? I suppose he is another of your daughter's friends, or your grand-daughter's?"* The ignorant creatures couldn't conceive that any patient in that ward could possibly be acquainted with a person of prominence in the outside world. And there was your poor little grandmother, who didn't even have her glasses on, peering at the paper and nodding her head because, as a matter of fact, although she could not recall the name, she did recognise the picture. She did know the person in question.'

'Oh, really? Who was it?' For the first time Laura looked genuinely interested.

'Oh, the name doesn't matter,' Ada said impatiently. 'It's slipped my own mind for the moment. But you should have seen with what civility she was treating those ill-bred creatures, with what dignity she was comporting herself –' Here Ada was overcome by an access of anguish. 'Oh, Laura, how could I have put her in that place? How could I have abandoned her, left her at the mercy of such people? The other patients could give her no consolation. They were moribund old women for the most part, comatose. They were no fit company for her. How she must have missed all the fascinating people you brought to the house when you were still living at home. She loved company. And what good company she was herself when she was on form. But those nurses – oh, they were foxy. When they saw me, those were the very words they used to try to cover up their callousness. "She's such good company," they said. "Such good fun." Fun?'

Laura said nothing for a moment. Then she put her hand

on Ada's and stroked it gently. 'Don't you think, Mummy, that a bit of fun might have been a welcome change in that ward – for all concerned?'

It was so sweet to have her daughter stroke her hand, Ada was prepared to compromise.

'I suppose I didn't think of it in that light. And of course your grandmother herself always appreciated light-hearted people.' But the next minute remorse returned and engulfed her. 'She must have been starved for companionship,' she said. Immediately Laura stopped stroking her hand.

'Oh, for God's sake, Mummy! Stop torturing yourself –'

'Torturing myself?'

'– and me!' Laura said. 'Oh, why can't you face it, grandmother *was* senile.'

The word was out at last, but Ada clapped her hands over her ears as if she was still in time to protect herself from hearing it.

'Thank God your poor grandmother can't hear you.'

'Don't be absurd! I would never have said such a thing in her hearing although, mind you, I think she might have cackled at the good of it. It's amazing how nature has cures for its own ills, and in her case the decay –'

'Decay?' Ada would have liked to block her ears again, but instead she retreated into herself. Wait till your own turn comes, miss! she thought. Then she had a wild impulse to yell this out, but she resisted. Instead tears flashed into her eyes, and although Laura despised tears, Ada could do nothing to stop them from falling. They splashed down on her hands.

'I'm sorry dear,' she murmured.

'Please, Mummy!' Laura was, as Ada expected, furious. Just

then, however, from Laura herself uncontrollably too, a sigh broke, sudden and loud like a hiccup, taking both of them by surprise.

Ada immediately took out her handkerchief and mopped her face. Laura walked over to the window.

Ada followed her daughter with her eyes. The garden was blazing with a sunlight that had gained in strength and brilliance since she'd looked out last. Ada had an urge to rush out at once in case that sun was too bright to last. But here Laura made a false move, heaving a second sigh which, unlike the first one, was not at all involuntary but of the deep and deliberate variety, intended perhaps to do for the heart what on occasion retching can do for the stomach – relieve it of too heavy a load.

'Mummy! For goodness' sake, come out to the garden,' she said, 'and show me how to take those cuttings. I'd love to be able to do it without depending on you.'

Ada thought that was a bit tactless for a daughter to say to a mother, but then Laura said something very nice.

'Would you believe it, Mummy, I never knew until the day of the sale, when I heard you telling the people who bought the house, that you yourself had propagated all those masses of pinks we had edging the paths in our garden at home. I always thought you'd bought them – paid a fortune for them!' Ada could not keep a smile from forming around her eyes and Laura quickly took advantage of it. 'Those masses of pinks were the bestest thing I've ever seen in any garden,' she said.

'Thank you, darling.' The babyish superlative her daughter had used was forever associated in her mind with the days when Laura was a tot, running around the old garden, gentle and biddable and seeming at times to float like thistledown among the flowers. Nevertheless, when her daughter proffered a hand to assist her to her feet, she brushed it away.

'I want you to know that I realise, of course, that in advanced age there is sometimes a diminution of powers, due to hardening of the arteries. But this doesn't necessarily impair the faculties, it just causes a momentary stoppage in the memory – a stoppage frequently unnoticed by the person herself, and often not noticeable to her listeners, either. The truth is that this can happen to anyone. And at any age!' There! Having got that off her chest Ada would have let the matter rest there, but Laura turned away as if the conversation was at an end, and started to look for something in a drawer of the sideboard, giving a distinct impression of dismissing everything that had been said between them that morning. Ada frowned. Surely that wasn't where they kept the garden clippers? And surely Laura knew you used your fingers to take a cutting? Ada's temper flared up again like a blaze through twigs. 'It may interest you to know, Laura,' she said, 'that hardening of the arteries has been known to set in as early as the mid thirties, or even the early thirties.'

Triumphant at last, Ada swept across the room to the glass door that led into the garden.

In the garden, however, she wasn't happy – not at all happy. For the remainder of the morning – and there wasn't much left of it – she was the one who was silent, while Laura chattered away uncharacteristically and almost inconsequentially, trying no doubt to make amends for her disagreeableness earlier. As usual, she overdid things. 'Are you sure it's all right for you to be working so hard?' she asked. As if work in a garden was ever easy! 'Why don't you take this fork, it's lighter.' As

if a light fork was of any use! And when they went inside
for lunch and Laura asked if she'd like a cushion behind her
back, Ada lost her temper.

'Ah, leave me alone,' she said, whereupon, of course, Laura
got huffy.

'I don't see why you object that your daughter – your
only child – should venture to suggest you might be
well advised to realise your age and take better care of
yourself!'

'That depends on what you mean by care?' Ada said
cautiously.

'Well, for one thing, you might consider having a check-up,'
Laura said, her candid eyes betraying no awareness of the
impertinence of this suggestion.

'In my opinion,' Ada said irritably, 'having a medical
check-up is only looking for trouble.'

'Sometimes a slight adjustment can help to avoid trouble
later on – major trouble,' Laura said ominously.

'But surely that is my business?' Ada said.

'Is it?'

'Yes, it is,' Ada said, quite simply, and to her astonishment
Laura was quelled. They proceeded amicably enough with the
lunch after that, although when they went out again Laura
was a lot less talkative. Ada didn't mind because, as the late
afternoon sun gilded the flowers and gave them a deeper
glow, her thoughts returned to her own garden and dwelt
there. By evening, she had paid the price of this indulgence.
She was saturated with sadness. So, at dusk, when John got
home, she was glad to go indoors with the young people. As
she hurried upstairs to change for supper, she could hear the
others talking in their own room, and listening to the sound

of their voices she was taken out of herself and restored to a happier frame of mind.

While she was running a comb through her hair, as a last-minute touch preparatory to going down, Laura came into her room without knocking.

'Look here, Mummy!' she said, without preamble. 'Perhaps if you won't listen to me, you will listen to John! He agrees with me. He thinks there may well be nothing wrong with you, but he says you owe it to me to see a doctor, just to put my mind at rest about you. He says you have a duty to me in this respect.'

Ada turned away in annoyance. So Laura had betrayed her? Such disloyalty from one's own flesh and blood was staggering. Daughter or no daughter, at that moment what Ada felt towards Laura was pure hatred. She would dearly have liked to give her a slap. Since one could not very well give a grown woman a slap, she was suddenly inspired to take a swipe at John.

'If your husband is so fond of doctors,' she said, enunciating each syllable with deadly precision, 'then why doesn't he get his antrums cleaned out? That, if you like, is a slight operation, hardly to be called an operation at all, except that it is a fairly painful business, I believe, because it has to be done without an anaesthetic. I'd say it would be worth it, though, if it put a stop to that ugly sniffling and snuffling of his – especially at night. Not that I mind, although if I did, I'd be in no position to complain, would I?' Here, however, Ada's venom shamed even herself and inwardly she collapsed. Outwardly she kept up a good front. 'Don't expect me to go down to dinner after this,' she said, 'I'm not much good at pretence!'

No sooner had she said this, however, than Ada realised

how little she'd eaten at lunch due to being upset then too. She had been literally starving since mid-afternoon. She hadn't really expected Laura to take her at her word. When the girl stalked out Ada's only consolation was to rush over to the door, and bang it shut. Then she sat down on the side of the bed and began to go back over what she was still determined to regard as accidents. Why did they happen?

Painstakingly, she tried to find a cause for each case. Since the first time, she had been taking the obvious precaution of cutting down her intake of fluids, especially towards evening. Ruefully, she remembered how, when she was first married, Patrick used to be amazed at the quantities of water she drank in the course of a day. As well as that, she used to bring a carafe of water up to their bedroom at night, a carafe which she would empty to the last drop before morning without any ill consequences. She was young then, of course, but surely if her kidneys had developed a weakness since then, it would have made itself manifest by day as well as by night? But no, she never suffered any inconvenience whatever during the daytime, neither on long journeys nor at the theatre, whereas some of her contemporaries could on occasion be a real nuisance. What then was the matter? She ate well. She slept well. Furthermore, sleep usually brought with it a proliferation of dreams – a sign of a sound mind in a sound body, or so she understood, having been told that it was firmly established by modern medics that in their dreams people got rid of their hang-ups. Her own dreams were always diverting – vivid and crammed with incident. And since she had come to live with Laura she had been keeping a pencil and pad on her bedside table to jot down as much as she could remember of a dream immediately on waking, because John enjoyed hearing her relate them. Ah, well! She'd better try to put her problem out of her mind for this night, and get into bed before she became so ravenous she would go down and make up with Laura.

When Ada settled herself between the sheets and switched off the bedside light, she was, at once, in the domain of dreams or, it would be more correct to say, she was at the gateway to that domain, because there was always a moment when, if a dream threatened to be disagreeable or scary, she could, at will, hold back and refuse to enter. But tonight the prospect that opened before her was full of wonder. She abandoned herself to it with joy.

To begin with, she was young again. And more joyous still, she was again with Laura's father.

'Oh, Patrick, did you hear what I called you?' she cried, because Laura could not possibly have been born then. They were on their honeymoon in the beautiful Villa Plaisance that a friend had lent them. Patrick laughed.

'Our baby may not be born yet, but she may be conceived,' he said, and they laughed for joy at the thought. And it might well have been true: they were two months married at the time, and nearing the end of their honeymoon. She knew this because, in the dream, Patrick had a time-table and was working out a schedule for their return journey. It might even have been their last day in Plaisance for, evidently not wanting to waste a second of the precious sun that poured down on the villa and surrounding country, they had decided to go outdoors and work on their schedule in a little wood behind the villa.

They had never been in this wood before – well, it wasn't exactly a wood, just a clump of trees that had no doubt been planted as a windbreak to keep the salt sea breezes from scorching the lawns. To their surprise, under the trees everywhere, the ground was carpeted with flowers like the forests in medieval tapestries. Not with primroses and bluebells, though, such as one might expect to find in a wood at home, but with cyclamens – myriads of rosy cyclamens. Neither she nor Patrick had ever seen such a breathtaking sight. At home wild flowers were soft, floppy, quick to wilt and spill their seeds, but these cyclamens looked hard as marble. Adamantine was the word that sprang to Ada's mind. She saw that on some of the corms the seeds that had already formed were raised up on wiry stems, tightly coiled and bent inward, as if to ensure an economy rather than a diffusion of seed. This colony of flowers was evidently of great antiquity. Some of the corms were so old and crusty they jutted over the ground like outcroppings of volcanic basalt. You couldn't walk through them without risk of twisting your ankle. At last, Patrick found a patch of thin grass and sat down; he produced the time-table, patting the ground beside him.

'Sit down, Ada. There's plenty of room. Sit down,' he said.

Ada was just about to sit down when at that moment she experienced a most irritating need of nature, un petit besoin as the French neatly put it.

'Just a second, Patrick! Sorry for being a nuisance, I'll have to run back to the house,' she said.

'Whatever for?' Patrick stared at her. She wasn't shy with him about something so natural, but she had noticed that he himself was reticent, or should she say respectful, of these small privacies, so she didn't answer. But he guessed.

'Why trudge back?' He pointed to the trees and laughed. 'What are trees for?'

'Oh Patrick!' She laughed too, but she was uneasy because, in the queer way that things switch in dreams, the trees had become sparse and spindly, and offered no concealment. The villa, on the other hand, had come close and it seemed to be all windows. If anyone looked out she would be seen distinctly. But by now the need to relieve herself was so pressing she had no choice but to run.

'Over there! Quick! Behind those laurels,' Patrick said, and she made for the cover, stumbling over the corms and treading the flowers into the ground. But now, everything had altered and the cyclamens were no longer real flowers, but glittering trinkets sharply edged and strong. They came to no harm under her feet.

Barely in time she reached the laurels, and pulled up her skirt. Oh, what bliss it was when the warmth of the sun was merged with a new warmth that rose up in vapour from the ground and seemed to bathe her whole body with moisture.

Oh God! Ada woke with a start. She sprang out of bed, but it was too late, and she sank down on the side of the bed. It was broad daylight and downstairs she heard the clatter of cups. The others were already at breakfast. Frantically, she wondered if she dared steal out on to the landing to see if the door of the linen closet might by chance have been left unlocked; she could snatch a pair of clean sheets, and bundle the others somewhere out of sight until she could get them to a laundry. But immediately she abandoned this hopeless project. Instead she went down on her knees and covered her face with her hands.

'Lord, Lord,' she prayed. 'Don't make it too hard on me.' Then suddenly, uncovering her face, she got to her feet and went over to the window. Drawing back the curtains, she stood looking down into the garden. Then, without kneeling, she amended her prayer. 'Don't make it too hard on Laura, I mean.'

JULIA O'FAOLAIN

Lots of Ghastlies

H er mother's now was a triple-layered face: icing-bright make-up dabs bobbed, brave as bunting, upon tides of fat and, somewhere beneath, foundered the shrewd, pretty, barfly's features. Only the Cupid's-bow lips were still the same: eager and shiny as when they used to kiss Priss quick, distracted good-nights. ('Comi-i-ing, you lot! Won't be a sec! Just gotta say goodnight to the . . . Be a good girl now, Priss. Say your prayers. Sleep tight!' And out of the door to the gang in the car, leaving behind her a waft of gin-and-lime and Amour-Amour.) She'd had to go on the wagon years ago.

'This neon's awful,' said Priss with depression.

'Oh?' said her mother. 'Everyone has it for the kitchen. What do they use in Italy?'

'This, too, I expect. I mean it's hard on the face.'

Her mother looked at her. 'It's true you've gone off,' she said. 'Since — how long since you were here? Four years? Five?'

163

'Three and a half,' said Priss. '*Because* I was out of the country.'

'Well, whatever life you've been leading, it's aged you. A little flesh keeps the skin smooth after thirty. You've got bags under your eyes.' The glance slid downward. 'What happened to your bust?'

'Busts are Out.'

Her mother's eye continued to descend and reached the bowl in which Priss was stirring eggs. 'What', her voice kited up, then was controlled, 'are you doing with ALL those eggs? THREE?'

'Making mayonnaise for supper. I saw you had salad in the fridge and Daddy's always liked mayonnaise.'

'With THREE eggs! Are you MAD?'

In a storm, the old groove-lines in her mother's face could not control the new yeastiness. This was a storm. Her flesh bubbled. She seized the bowl from Priss but then did not know what to do with it. She considered the vulnerable, quaking yolks, which could not now be restored to their shells, and paused.

'Goodness, I'll pay you for them if you like!'

'Pay! That's a nice one! Ha! From you!'

'Oh . . .'

'The way you paid back the hundred pounds I sent you to get married with!'

'Ten years ago, for God's sake!'

'Stop swearing! And did you get married? I suppose you'd never expected to? Pay – you may live in luxury with your rich friends. Mayonnaise, caviar no doubt . . . You have the tastes . . . Eggs cost . . .'

'Mother!'

'Don't address me in that tone. You're irresponsible. You couldn't even keep your own child – what did happen to her?'

'Peregrine? She's been adopted. You won't be asked to lay out anything for her.'

'Poor child.. . .' Her mother sniffled. 'I suppose I'll never see her now . . .'

'You never wanted to before . . .'

Her mother had seen something in the sink. 'The WHITES!' she shouted. 'You threw them away! THREE whites! Down the drain!'

The sniffles had turned to sobs. Her mother let herself fall on to a hard-backed kitchen chair. 'It's so typical,' she wailed. 'I don't know . . . I've always wanted things to be nice between us . . .'

Priss took off her apron and walked back to the living-room. Her father cocked an eye up from the television.

He whispered: 'A little drinky?'

'Should you?'

He closed the eye. He was no older than Bandino, who still zipped around Europe in racing cars and could polish off a magnum of champagne any night of the week. Or topple a bird when Priss's back was turned. She filled two glasses. Her father grinned, then winked again. 'Bottoms up!' His eye boomeranged back to the TV programme: a cricket match. There was a bounce in him still. He'd always been a great one for ball games: rugby, golf, even croquet. She remembered grassy afternoons and a triumphant flow of liquor as he whisked balls through hoops and into holes. 'Not bad, what? Got to keep my end up with you chaps!'

A ricocheting laugh. He'd been a bookie, though she told Bandino and all her London friends that he was 'an Army man'. They imagined a tight-lipped officer whose behaviour when she'd first slipped from the path of virtue precluded her return to it. ('Brought up strictly, kicked over the traces . . .' It was neat and satisfying. Like his wink.) In fact, she couldn't remember his behaviour. There hadn't been any. He had been indifferent, absorbed in her mother who, then as now, had wept over things turning out less nicely than she had anticipated. Her maternal tears flowed with the ease of juice from a plastic lemon. She had been a plucked-browed beauty, toast of the golf club, swaying in the sun on ginny dappled afternoons as he cocked his shots. Plip! Plop! 'A neat poke! Cheers!'

And now he sits glued to the telly while I cavort around Europe with old Bandino. I should get him a girl. One of my friends. Miranda, perhaps, or even Catherine. He has charm and an older man makes you feel young. Better to be young flesh for someone else than to be on the prowl for it. I mean for a woman. At thirty-two one is in between. Poor Daddy watching his little screen: a shrunken world. He used to be such a great juicy man, all strawberry and ginger colours. He had a sweet smile as if his teeth were coloured by a film of honey. But rarely for me: a lanky sprat in convent uniform. How old was I – eleven? – the Sunday morning I went into their bedroom. The char hadn't come for some reason and I had been waiting for my breakfast for hours. There was a powerful shaft of sunlight coming through the curtains on to the bed and I saw them doing something astonishing – I hadn't the faintest idea what. Indeed, I forgot about it for years. What I remembered was his fury and the way he leaped up, carelessly naked, pink and quivering with rage, to order me out of their room. 'Out!' A thunderclap. Rigid pointing finger. A hairy, gold-glinting God-the-Father condemning curiosity, when all I'd wanted was my breakfast and not to be left alone so long in my room. 'Your room!' he shouted. 'Go to your room!' And off I slunk, wrapped in my Teddy-bear dressing-gown and not understanding a thing.

'Prissy!'

He was looking at her from under still-ginger brows. 'Another gin?'

'If *you* do.'

He held up the bottle in a way she had seen her mother do, tracing the liquid-line with a finger-nail.

'She marks it,' he murmured.

Oh, Lord! Why? His liver? But we all have livers. Bandino has. He takes pills and visits the fashionable spas but drinks like a fish. Says he wants to go out with a bang. Or – could it be because I was coming? I, with my baggy eyes and indeterminate status.

'Better keep the bottle out of sight while she's around, dear!'

So they think I'm a lush! And irresponsible. I brought a daughter into the world and don't devote myself to her! *She'd* like to see me tied down among nappies, feed-bottles, potties, and plastic teething things! Oh, yes. Revenge. A lousy mother she was, too! Peregrine has a nice adoptive one: broody and barren. Big-bosomy Sarah, born to the role. One should always have I.B.M.-linked mother teams: 'Sexy, fertile producer seeks good child-rearer.' Peregrine shall judge. No, she shall not. She'll probably grow up to be something depressing like a lady don when I've joined the Light Brigade of old English bags one sees propped about the gaming tables in places like Deauville, getting my last chancy pleasures in a game of chemmy. 'Oh, my mama', she'll say of me with a giggle, 'is such a character . . .' Meanwhile, I'll have a wanton drink with my treacherous old Dad.

She poured him a stiff one. He examined it with some alarm.

'Come on, Daddy! Never say die!'

His laugh again. Golden hairs on the hand that tapped her knee.

'You're a bad lot, Prissy.'

If I weren't his daughter now he'd pinch my bottom. If I were just some still-youngish bird. As I am: not quite a boiler yet, for all my eye-bags. I can look damn well if I go off the liquor for a week or two, or even if I don't, I can look damn well with the proper make-up and hair-do. God, though, I used to be so marvellous-looking *all* the time and now . . . Oh, that night last April when Peregrine's father – when *Paul* – turned up at a dinner-party and I introduced him to Bandino! I had been looking forward to seeing him again, even though he did behave like a bastard, and I wanted to let him see I was with someone as grand as he – he always was a snob – and to let Bandino meet him for the same reason. I knew Paul's wife would be there but I felt no interest. She had been the reason Paul wouldn't acknowledge Peregrine, but that was water under the bridge and wives – '*Mesdames les légitimes*', as that girl from Lyons, what was her name, used to call them – are better not thought about. Paul had been crazy about me. Everyone said so, and said that if that sort of provincial aristocrat ever did break loose, he would have for me. In our story I was the beautiful and the damned so, by all the rules, she must be a homely country mouse, mustn't she? And then . . . this magnificent brilliant bird appeared – oh, an apparition – in an Ungaro dress, looking as though every bit of her had been put together by hand: a unique, *hors série*, top-designer creation; clever, too, speaking four or five languages – it was that sort of dinner – and looking ten years younger than me. I saw Bandino's eyes rolling toward her and Paul's shock at the sight of drooping me. Oh, yes! '*Où sont nos amoureuses?/Elles sont au tombeau./Elles sont plus heureuses/Dans un séjour plus beau . . .*' A convenient arrangement. I would have liked to have been in the *tombeau* that evening and I felt Paul would have preferred me there, too. A painful session. Lots of ghastlies. Oh, well.

'A penny for them, Priss?'

'They're not worth it.'

'Drink up,' invited her father surprisingly. 'A little of what you fancy', he put on a comic accent, 'does you good!'

Ha! The liquor is warming him, bringing him back from the tomb. That's what he needs more of. Better to die roaring than whining. Think of the aids and props Paul and Bandino have: tapestried houses, dogs, pistols, Jaguars, birds. Daddy has to make do with his telly. And *she* goes berserk over the loss of three egg whites. If I touched him now – as she did then – would he revive completely?

Her mother brought in an unnecessarily heavy tray, struggling. They both leaped.

'Mother, you should have called. Let me take it.'

'Well, if you want to!' Relinquishing it without grace: 'Hardly worth it at this point.'

She'd cooked, or rather fixed, a meal: beans on toast,

sausages, beer. No sign of the mayonnaise. No salad. A deliberately depressing, austerity meal. As if to remind Priss what she had come from and let her not forget it: poor-but-honest; plain-and-decent. Untrue. All those golf and tennis clubs must have cost a packet. Not to mention the liquor. In the old bookie and nookie days when Priss was packed off to boarding-school, insulated in coarse woollen underwear, she'd had it good. Priss didn't grudge it to her. She *wanted* her to have it good, for God's sake.

'I'm afraid this is dull fare for Priss!' Her mother cast her into the semi-absence of the third person.

Did they *like* her visiting? They groused when she stayed away but perhaps preferred their grouse? Or were they pleased but had forgotten how to show it?

'But I *adore* bangers!' she said. Which sounded – Jesus!

'How long can you stay?' her mother asked.

Play this by ear! Bandino was supposedly in Scotland with people who, knowing his wife, could not sanction Priss. Shooting birds. Not his favourite activity with birds, though he was capable even of that! Anyway, he was to pick her up on Tuesday at the local town where he had dropped her off today. But – should she stay here till Tuesday?

'I'm afraid I upset your routine.'

'Oh, don't consider *us*!' said her mother.

'We see so little of you,' said her father.

Now that was warm! Wasn't it? It was.

'Darlings,' said she. It wasn't their sort of word but it was *her* sort and she felt spontaneous suddenly. Better display this surge of affection before it ebbed. '*Darlings*! It is super to be with you a bit and you are looking marvellous. Both of you!' She squeezed his wrist and knew she should do something of the same sort to her mother, too; but her mother was on her left – a sluggish side of her – and the bread-board had got in between, and her mother's right hand was defensively busy with food, so she didn't. Damn!

He raised his tankard and crinkled his eyes at her over the rim.

I really like Englishmen best: that restrained humour of theirs as they play you along, casting slowly like sensual fishermen. They can seethe and steam, too. Only they have no sex myth, which is a pity. I mean, vim for vim, it's often their picture of themselves as cocks that keeps men going. Look at Bandino. He talks much more than he performs nowadays. But he talks very well. And his seductions are mostly for show.

Did Daddy, I wonder, ever step out on my mother?

'To us,' said her father, drinking his beer.

Her mother made a little stabbing movement with her glass. She couldn't drink now because of her diabetes. This time Priss caught her hand as she put it down. Her mother let her hand be held, then relinquished. It was an inconclusive gesture.

But I would like, thought Priss, to be warm with her.

She helped her father wash up. 'Why don't we nip out to the local?' she suggested. 'When we finish this.'

Her father looked worried. 'Your mother', he reminded her, 'can't drink. She doesn't like pubs any more, either.'

'Well, you and I could slip out for a quick one. Just be about forty minutes.' But she knew it was a brisk fifteen minutes' walk each way and they would hardly be content with ten minutes in the pub. Still, she wanted very much to go. She thought of the hedges they would pass. They were

JULIA O'FAOLAIN

made up of rank wild greenery: alder and nettles and dock, and the prospect of plunging into the tunnelly lanes excited her. She had been abroad so long with Bandino that she felt the green English rural twilight would refresh her like a swim in lake water. Her father had always liked walking. They would stride quickly – because of getting back to her mother – bouncing on the ball of the foot along rubbery ground, not dusty as in Italy, nor concrete as in London, but ground that was responsive to the step. Like Antaeus, she would be restored. Then there would be the mild gleam of the pub. 'Let's,' she insisted.

'No,' said her father. 'Oh, I'm afraid', he giggled, 'I've had too much already. Not used to it, you know. Feel tiddly.'

So they returned to the living-room where her mother was watching the television.

'Look', said she, 'at that' – it was a London fashion show – 'I won't say "indecency", because what is indecent nowadays, but at the sheer silliness of women over thirty wearing skirts that short!'

'They call them "pussy pelmets",' said Priss, who had cautiously worn her longest skirt for this trip into the provinces. But she felt got at. She was sure her mother had guessed she was a trendy dresser.

'It's all right', her mother went on, 'for teenagers. Rather sweet on them, in fact! I remember you had a sweet little kilt from the Scotch House when you were fifteen. Way above your knees, even though it wasn't the fashion then. That was 1956,' she stated precisely. She looked back at the screen. 'Now it suits her,' she nodded approvingly at a pale waif in what looked like a plastic gymslip. 'She must be about seventeen, wouldn't you say? Still boyish. It's these old things of thirty flattening down their breasts and wearing their hems above their bottoms that would make a cat laugh! How can they expect any man to take them seriously? They're neither children nor adults. Nothing.'

'Oh, the men like it.' Priss told her. 'For the first time Englishmen are turning round in the street to look at women. Just like in France or Italy. The very first time. The décolletés never got them. They're leg men.'

Her mother snorted. 'They may *look*!' she said, 'but do they *marry*?'

Oh, hell! Still trying to knock me sexually. Is she jealous of me or disappointed for me? If this is the way mother love curdles, it's a good thing I gave up Peregrine. Maybe it's because I didn't want to turn into a replica of *her* that I never married? Paul wouldn't have married me and Bandino won't, but Jeremy would have, like a shot, and that sweaty millionaire, and Michael, who is probably going to be a peer. God, the chances I've turned down. And I'm *nice* to men: patient and good-humoured and adaptable. There've been so many. I've *had* to be. And I'm not possessive or jealous at all! Whereas all she's ever been is spoiled and cosseted. A one-man-for-one-woman arrangement is inhuman. It should be stopped. She has him so utterly under her thumb!

He was fussing with his pipe.

'I think this new generation', her mother was saying, 'is a great improvement on the last. The teens I mean. They're more imaginative.'

'Well,' said Priss, 'people usually get on better with their grandchildren, don't they, than with their own children.'

'I don't know what you're insinuating!'

'Nothing,' said Priss. 'Unless', it occurred to her, 'that

you're using the teeny-bopper generation as a stick to beat mine with.'

'Who mentioned yours? You are touchy, I must say! How can you know what's going on in my mind?'

'Is it so obscure?'

'Don't be insolent,' said her mother. 'You're obviously loaded with complexes and the sense of failure. I'm sorry for you.'

'Why do you provoke me like that?' Priss asked her.

'*Me* provoke you? Honestly! That's a good one.' Her mother laughed theatrically. 'Did you hear that, Edwin?' she appealed to Priss's father.

Puffing at his pipe, he gave no sign of having paid any attention to what had been said.

'I . . .' the mother began again.

'Oh, drop it, will you?' said Priss. 'I've taken all I can take.'

'You've taken all you can take!' shouted her mother. 'Will you listen to that, Edwin, from your precious daughter? Will you? She can't set foot in this house, even after being away four years, without being offensive! It's intolerable. I don't ask what she's been doing. I'd rather not know. Although I've a good enough idea. And so have the neighbours. I can tell by the way they ask after her. And then getting you drunk and baiting me . . . yes, baiting! I can't stand it! I can't! From that – whore!' She began to sob violently.

Priss's father put down his tobacco pouch as though giving up a weapon. 'Now, Roslyn,' he patted his wife's shoulder, 'pull yourself together. It's a little misunderstanding. That's all. She gets upset,' he told Priss. 'You must try not to upset her. It's those drugs she takes', he smiled vaguely, 'for the diabetes.' On the furry hearth rug, with the lamplight glinting on the hair of his hand, he looked furry himself: a domesticated animal.

'I think', said Priss, 'I'll spend the night at the pub. I'll ring you in the morning. I'm sorry. No, I'm sure. Yes, I remember the taxi number. You stay here.'

She telephoned a taxi from the hall, then went into the loo to comb her hair and put on lipstick. Her overnight bag was still by the front door where she had left it. It was uncompromisingly small. Had she ever meant to stay?

He came out to say good-bye. She must be sure to ring in the morning. 'Mother will feel differently,' he assured her. 'She hasn't been quite herself . . . Will you be all right alone?'

'Darling! In the English countryside? Of course! I'm a nightbird, you know!'

He took her out to the taxi and stuck his head through the window to kiss her good-bye. Then he withdrew it, bounced back up the porch steps, and flipped a hand along some hanging bamboo chimes in a gesture of spry farewell. Before the driver had managed to turn his vehicle in the narrow drive, the door had closed behind him and the hall light snapped on. Seconds later, Priss sighted his silhouette in the landing window turned away from her to engage in a pantomime of comic relief. With something much too large to be a handkerchief – a table-runner perhaps? – he sponged his brow and flung out his arms with the old clubman's vivacity. Suddenly her mother was in them and the two, floating like a bright icon above the dark doorway, remained clinging in a still, utterly relaxed embrace until Priss's taxi had made its noisy exit down their gravelled drive.

BRIEGE DUFFAUD

Innocent Bystanders

The fire died with a soft splash and sigh of falling ash. Her mother was asleep in the armchair and Helen didn't like to disturb her by going out for more briquettes. It wasn't that cold anyhow. The daughter tried to read and the mother slept on, snoring very slightly. She dropped into sleep easily nowadays; no sooner had the Feeneys left than she settled into the chair and drifted off as if Helen was a thousand miles away. But then the Feeneys would put anyone to sleep, Helen thought, Father Joseph guzzling After Eights and lamenting the desperate changes he saw in Ireland – worse every time he came home, the country entirely given over to the punks and the layabouts. Not to mention the violence, his sister said, it's a holy terror that decent people can't come and go in peace in the town they were reared in, you wouldn't mind them shooting soldiers but the majority of the time it's innocent bystanders that's called on to suffer and what is Ireland coming to?

It had been the same refrain last time Helen was home, over fifteen years earlier, only then it was the miniskirt and the Beatles and how decent people couldn't even go out to Mass without having their eyes assaulted by shameless tramps showing everything they had. Pure vinegar, Miss Feeney, and always was. How in the name of God did Mother put up with her? They seemed to be the best of friends, though it had not always been so. But then Mother was shockingly changed, her standards were not the same. There was a slackening, a sort of quiet indifference that made impossible any but the most platitudinous attempt at conversation.

The violent changes round home did not touch Helen at all, she'd come prepared for them: where she lived now the very name of the town she'd grown up in had become a sort of shorthand for terror. What did shock her though was this unexpected picture of her mother in retirement. The slangy clichés holding life at a distance, Dallas on the telly, the synthetic plants and the flowery carpets and the Lourdes water bottled in fluorescent plastic. A Mills and Boon romance jostling the Rosary beads and on the same shelf a few library books and a motheaten copy of *Gone With the Wind*. Helen remembered that being hidden under the mattress long ago when it came in the Yankee parcel, for fear that Miss Feeney might drop in with her holy spying eyes and now here it was out in the open.

Things were changed all right: the very book she was reading, published in Dublin no less, some girl had an abortion in it and no one belonging to her as much as turned a hair! It couldn't have been written the last time she was home, wouldn't have got printed, would have been on the Index or something, Archbishop McQuaid thundering

177

from his pulpit. She was glad of course, oh she wasn't knocking it at all, only it was shutting her out, all this dream world, this JR and Crossroads and the splashy fitted carpets and the picture windows. Cur-rist! she thought, the old woman whatever her faults she used to at least talk about real things, she never quit instilling all the virtues into us both at home and at school. Not content with the patriotic trimmings to the Rosary she used to have the lot of us lined up in the classroom reciting 'The Rebel' and vowing that we'd do our level best to die for our country like Patrick Pearse who was her great idol. You started off in Infants with Miss Feeney drumming it into you that the only noble destiny was to be a foreign missionary risking your life in a heathen jungle like her own brother, then you got promoted to Mother's class and told what a proud thing it must be to die for Ireland. For your Faith too of course, she was stiff with ideals when I was a kid.

Or am I re-inventing her, Helen wondered, am I busy building myself a folklore? Well, she was stuck in the middle of more reality now than she ever bargained for and all she could do was cry over some American shit of a soap-opera and switch off the News with a sighed cliché about what was the world coming to at all at all? And drift off to sleep while her daughter waited in vain for the healing words, the anger and forgiveness, the slap followed by the blessing. Not a word had been spoken so far about Helen's situation, about the years of estrangement, there had been no prodigal's welcome. They went here and there to visit neighbours, exchanged harmless remarks, helped Miss Feeney arrange the house for her reverend brother's holiday. Sometimes Tim came over from Newry for the evening but that was awkward too; they had never got on well. He'd always been a scourge with his jokes and his jeers and now, heading for middle-age, his jokes had razor blades in them. A sour old bachelor. Helen, longing for intimacy, dying to spread out her life for the delight of her family, was forced to sit evening after evening nursing a book in front of a dead fire while her mother dozed. Yet she sent for me, Helen thought, she did send for me.

'You wouldn't know there was a bit of trouble in the country at all.' That's what her mother had written a month before. 'It's all quiet and peaceful around here, the odd explosion or kidnapping, but sure the half of the time you wouldn't hear a word about it till you saw it on the News.' She wrote as she spoke, had always done so. For two decades her words had brought without fail the handful of small rocky fields, the country schoolhouse, turf-bog spread at its feet, Slieve Gullion a distant blue hump, child's mountain-shape hiding no secrets. Brought them as balm or as blame, as ginny tears on a foreign beach, as iconoclastic intruders into a life that occasionally, and at last, promised freedom: this is all you are, this is where you'll end up. Her letters were constantly consoling, insulting, being proud of her clever daughter, ashamed of her, encouraging her, accusing her, twitching her back from the edge of adventure, plucking her out of the centre of some happiness, stopping her hand in the instant of caress. They were a rope, stupid old lifeline/umbilical cord, attaching Helen to her.

Only not to her, not to this woman Nellie McCabe, country schoolmarm, whom one knew to be ordinary, warm, funny, ignorant, as wise and as foolish as any woman, as fond of a laugh, of a new dress, a good meal – not to her at all, Helen wouldn't have minded, but to this great and sorrowing institution, The Irish Catholic Mother, and in her mother's case more: Irish Catholic Widowed Mother, with what that implied of martyrdom and sacrifice. Image of course of Our Immaculate Lady who's forever prying into one's mind and heart and going beetroot with shame at what her virgin eyes see there. But image and more so of Mother Erin, that poor unwilling battered wife with her trials and her tribulations, exalted by suffering to a monumental egoism, obsessed to the point of neurosis with her terror of being in the end betrayed by her faithless ungrateful offspring.

The rope had been left lying slack for seven years, ever since the news of Helen's second marriage. Indeed Helen had believed it cut, and had suffered accordingly. Her mother didn't write at all, not as much as a Christmas card or a line when Caroline was born. When Helen most needed letters, needed blame, praise, encouragement, some proof for godsake that she existed, that she was remembered with warmth by the handful of small fields, well then she didn't write. Helen wrote to her explaining, accusing (her intolerance, her narrow-mindness and what did you think I was anyway, a bloody nun?), insulting, begging, raging, until finally broken-backed with remorse and loneliness she began to crawl belatedly towards some semblance of maturity.

Then in September, the letter. She wasn't as young as she used to be, a body thinks things over, it was a pity to lose all contact, to keep up old disagreements. She supposed Helen was in the habit of going here and there for her holidays, would she not think of spending a week or two in Ireland sometime soon and bringing Caroline? There was no danger at all, she need have no worries about bringing the child, sure you'd never know there was a . . .

Though Helen knew otherwise – knew that all that Spring

and Summer one man after another had gone deaf and blind and mad with hunger, knew that young fellows who should be out kicking football, shifting girls in discos, making love, building homes and families, were sitting naked in bare rooms repeating other people's slogans, smearing and choking their minds with the left-over excrement of History – she allowed her mother's letter to speak to her only of the peace of small rocky fields, turf-bog spread lazily at their feet, child's drawing of mountain lying across the horizon, the neighbours so good with lifts and shopping and sure we'll meet you at the airport. The rope had twitched again pulling her back and, anaesthetised with gratitude, she asked no questions, let herself be pulled.

Driving down from the airport she had been warmed by the remembered prettiness of hill and hedgerow and old grey monastery, impressed by the new prosperity of bright little bungalows with white rail fences. 'Like a returned Yank!' Tim sneered, drawing her attention instead to the posters and the scrawled slogans, a photo of Mrs Thatcher with the caption: This Woman is a Mass Murderer. Do not attempt to apprehend her yourself: Call on the Provisional IRA.

'Witty!' Helen said, and Tim looked at her in unbelieving disgust.

Their mother, trying to make peace between them, had spoken of the Pope's visit, the great boost it had been for the morale of the country. 'I never thought I'd live to see our Holy Father here in Ireland, though indeed what country has a better right to welcome him after the centuries of martyrdom we endured for our Faith.'

'Then it's a pity he didn't come to the part needed him most,' Tim said. 'He made damn sure he didn't venture too far north. Here listen to this one, Helen: big broad clergyman, big broad Ballymena accent, "A'm tallin' yez, brethren, if they let thon lad across the border he'll not be kissin the groun', he'll be bitin' the dust!" ' Helen was on tenterhooks; in the past an irreverence like that would have earned him the flat of a hand across his jaw, but their mother didn't seem to notice, turned away with a vague smile to point out some big new tourist hotel. I suppose she's mellowing, Helen had thought at the time, she's getting on after all . . .

. . . A noise that she knew from the telly was the sound of a muffled explosion growled through the night, rattled the windows, lingered casually grumbling between the walls for a while, became part of the dark. 'There's the Barrack away up in smoke!' her mother said flippantly as though she had never been asleep. Helen had a mad and desolate vision of floodlit bodies being hurtled mercilessly towards the stars (tell us, Mister Einstein luv, how long is an instant when you're being blown apart?).

'Oh do you think . . .' half rising from her chair with a helpful St John's Ambulance face.

'N-o-o-t at all child, troth and you'd know all right if it was the Barrack, you wouldn't be sitting there so cool. It was the wrong direction anyhow, I'd say that was somewhere up the Dundalk road, some old patrol or another. We'll hear the hellys in a minute taking off to investigate.' They did. 'Some poor mothers' sons for all that,' she mourned, atoning for the flippancy and Helen said, because there was nothing to say, 'I'm afraid I let the fire die down. Will I get you a cardigan?'

'If you wouldn't mind,' she said, 'the old Aran in the wardrobe and I'll make us a wee cup of tea and a biscuit.'

Helen checked that Caroline had not been woken then went to her mother's room, stumbling across the sheepskin rug to draw the curtains before she put the light on because the night before two blackened faces had leered in at her, pressed up against the pane. They lay up in the ditches all night, her mother said, or in some cattle shelter in the corner of the field and were picked up by helicopter in the early morning. Whatever they expected to find in a retired widow's flowerbeds . . . Must be unnerving, she thought, alone here night after night and me in a foreign country and Tim living miles away. She knew that was the whole problem. She had known it even while she raged at her mother asleep and remote from her. It's not me she's shutting out at all, she thought, it's them out there, and the screeches of the random dead, and all the heroes and the villains and the sly boys lining their pockets and every poor fool that ever dreamed of lying up in a tri-coloured coffin clasping a bunch of lilies in his stainless marble hand. And could you blame her?

A neighbour fellow got taken from his house a while back, was jostled into a stolen car, tried by a People's Court and executed – his unfortunate corpse booby-trapped left lying in the road like an abandoned car waiting for some poor cod of a paramedic trooper to try taking his pulse. An informer. The green green grass of home, Tim called him and even that didn't earn him a clout on the gob. They were at school with him, Helen and Tim both and she taught him. He'd have been part of the line-up reciting Pearse. She recalled him as a bit of a slabber, knew it all, all the ins and outs, all the local gossip. An informer though? Walking self-righteously straight-backed up to ring the Barrack doorbell or whispering secrets to some slimy blackguard in the corner of a pub? Hard to imagine but then who can you trust these days? That's what she must be thinking, or not thinking, floating into sleep, spending her well-known Christian charity on the griefs of some actress or another, you knew where you were with the telly and the love stories, they wouldn't turn round and repeat some innocent peevish remark to the boys. And the handsome blue-chinned hero wouldn't ever turn out to be Captain Nairac looking for news.

Her things were hanging up neatly in the wardrobe: coats, jackets, dresses. And there in the middle of them, cleaned and pressed and well looked-after was the grey flannel coat Helen had bought her in Paris thirteen years earlier. It was the same one all right, silk label discreetly flaunting itself. If she'd thought about it at all Helen would have expected it to be thrown out years ago, slashed to rags, given to some gypsy at the very least. Her mother's rages used to be like that: destroy the better to forgive. Helen was gathered up and wrung breathless in the grip of an instant's hate, image following merciless image of half-buried injustices, tyranny, intolerance, then she relaxed and stretched herself deliberately in the warmth of other memories.

To think that she kept the coat, cared for it, obviously wore it from time to time! There was a scarf twisted round the neck, not a great match, she'd buy her another when they went to Newry tomorrow, blue-grey silk, gentle and undramatic as the sky over Slieve Gullion. They'd go here and there sightseeing and they'd eat in one of the big tourist hotels; she used to thrive on that sort of outing years ago. Helen recalled the day her mother came tearing up to Belfast intent on murder and instead they went to dine in the Pig 'n' Chicken and Helen forced her to eat asparagus because it was the dearest vegetable on the menu and she came out in a rash that disfigured her for weeks. She never let on she was allergic to it because Helen was treating her and because she was feeling guilty at having listened to backbiting gossip about her daughter.

Helen was nineteen then, working in the Civil Service after being expelled from teacher training college for going to London with a Protestant student to take part in an Africa Freedom march, and they'd told her mother, someone had written to her, some jealous cow, that Helen was still going around with the Prod and attending Socialist meetings and everything, and she went in a terrible state to Belfast, fully intending to pull the hair out of her daughter's head and boot her down home like some Edna O'Brien heroine in front of the countryside. Only the landlady talked to her for an hour before Helen got in from work and assured her that there wasn't one word of truth in the report, that she was a good-living wee girl well settled down now after the shaking-up she got, going to her religious duties regular and running up to St Teresa's Hall every Sunday night like all the rest to dance with nice Catholic boys from Andersonstown and in no time at all she'd be married to some schoolteacher or bank man and before Mrs McCabe knew where she was she'd be nursing a clatter of grandchildren aye missus ah'm tallin' ye! So instead of a row they went to see Doreen Hepburn in the Arts Theatre and Helen took her out to dinner in a posh restaurant and everything was easy and friendly. Except that her mother came out in a rash. And, because she'd kept the coat Helen felt that things would be easier now too, the distance that separated them would go, they'd be able to talk together the way they used to. In spite of the years of silence she'd kept it, she'd worn it, that was surely some indication of her state of mind, of the affection there still was between them.

Four years after the Belfast episode Helen was married and separated, working in Paris, her husband left behind in London. 'No reconciliation is possible, Mammy,' she wrote. 'Don't even suggest I go back to that man!' Her mother went flying over, one hand full of Mass Bouquets for her intentions, the other raised ready to batter her back to respectability. Helen said she was well battered already, threw off her clothes to show the scars and the half-faded bruises, said she'd stuck a whole year of that and Sacrament or no Sacrament she had no intention of going back. By that time her mother was crying over her and saying: 'Well the blaggard! Well I always said he was nothing only a pup! Well the jumped-up beggar's get, I'll settle him for good and all!' When she stopped crying and calmed down she said Helen was perfectly right and wasn't it a sensible decision to leave London, he'd never think of looking for her across the Channel. Helen said there was no danger of him sending out search parties, he was fixed up already, no shortage of willing ladies in swinging London and no doubt as soon as the divorce went through he'd get to work on some other poor innocent. Her mother said a divorce wouldn't be much advantage to Helen and was she sure the marriage had been consummated properly because if not they could start applying straight away for an annulment. Helen asked wouldn't the scars do and her mother said no, violence was considered a natural hazard of marriage but any inability to perform his duties would be a different matter entirely. Helen said it was consummated all right but thanks be to God she wasn't pregnant or anything. Her mother said indeed it was nothing to be thankful for, it was a terrible pity because she had a long lonely life before her now and what a mistake it was to rush foolishly into marriage like that and unless he died young Helen had forfeited any chance of having a home of her own and children.

'But,' she said, 'you can always count on me in any problems or difficulties, I'll always be there and you have a good home waiting for you whenever you need it. Though,' she added, 'it might be best not to go back to Ireland yet awhile with the sort of nosy neighbours we have, it'd do old Feeney's heart good to see you in the middle of another scandal!'

Helen hadn't wanted to go home then anyway. She was free and the world was wide. She was so relieved at her mother's attitude and to tell the truth so happy at seeing her that she rushed her off to a famous boutique where they were having a sale and found her this lovely grey coat and spent the two months' wages on it that she'd saved up to go to Cuba with. Her mother loved the coat and never stopped talking about the cut of it and the simplicity and it was the nicest thing she ever owned and nothing would do her but to rig Helen out from the same shop, she was a holy show with the face of some hooligan pop star plastered across her chest, a married woman in a tragic situation it was neither right nor proper to be dolling herself up like a teenager.

Helen told her it was no pop star, that was Che Guevara she said, it was the face of a saint Mammy, a real saint, they were after killing him in Bolivia fighting for the cause of the poor and the oppressed and couldn't she see it wasn't a pop star, pop singers didn't look like that, the dedication, the nobility and didn't her mother think he looked more like a sort of Jesus Christ I mean the way Jesus probably did look Mammy not the awful holy pictures and her mother drew back and would have lifted her hand to her only she remembered in time they were in public. She said don't ever say a thing like that Helen not even in a joke, Our Blessed Lord was wise and gentle and peaceful at all times and killed or no killed yon thing was more like some of the heroes you'd see propping up Murphy's corner on a Dole day.

Helen told her every single person in Paris, my God, Mammy, even old people like Yves Montand and Sartre, venerated this guy and everyone was wearing his face on their sweater and quoting from his book every single person Mammy, and the crowds surged in and out of the boutique with his face on their bags and scarves humming 'Duerme Negrito' and 'Changuito Guerrillero', and her mother laughed and said oh my a my the latest from Paris, you were always the great one for following fashion! Helen tried to explain that she was changed, that she was more mature now and it wasn't just fashion, fashion had nothing got to do with it, the way people everywhere were changing their natures because of the example of this one fab human being and soon there'd be a whole new race of mankind wise and compassionate and brave who'd be ready to drop everything, he was a doctor Mammy imagine a qualified doctor, and go off to fight injustice anywhere in the world.

And her mother said Helen was to be sure and send her a postcard when that happened and new man or no new man he still looked like some cornerboy. They had a bitter argument there in the shop, Helen trying to convince her, and her mother said she was making a show of herself in front of the people and to come on out for heaven's sake.

All the same they had a great week, it was the last time they enjoyed themselves together, it was the last time they saw each other till now. In the end she went home in the lovely coat saying her daughter's happiness would always be the first intention in her prayers and that she was glad anyway Helen was fitted up with a good decent job and please God she'd make some suitable friends and above all she was to keep pure and good and resist temptation. As an Irish Catholic she was in a special position and had a duty to set an example to everyone she came across. She shoved a wad of Novena leaflets into Helen's pocket and the address of a Legion of Mary group that she'd got from the concierge, the pair of them having struck up a friendship whose vocabulary consisted of words like Lourdes, Lisieux, Cluny and which, Helen knew, had destroyed any chance of a private life for her, she'd have to move digs. She couldn't stop crying on the coach back from the airport; it came to her that her whole life long, since the evening she got dumped in the Convent, her mother was constantly going home to warmth and shelter and leaving her alone in some horrible place to cope with things. Then she stopped crying and went to give her evening classes at the Berlitz . . .

'. . . Can you not find it? Sure take any old cardigan and come on, your tea's wet and everything.'

She had the fire started up again with a couple of firelighters and a whole heap of briquettes, the waste of it so near bedtime, but lovely and welcoming to take the last bit of chill off Helen's memories. The coffee table with the fancy tiled top was pulled up on the hearthrug with pink marshmallow biscuits and a plate of bread for toasting. It was neat and bright and homely. Helen thought of her own basement flat with its constant smell of damp from the river and its chronic untidiness and all of a sudden she wanted desperately to be let stay, to let her life slide gently, unquestioningly, between teacup and telly, all the neat little truths lined up in order, with Heaven swept and dusted waiting at the end. She wanted more than anything for her mother to say: 'Sure I can see you're not happy at all over there and why need you go back when there's a good home waiting for you here.' But her mother gave no cue at all and the moment passed, as it always had. Helen commented on the nice cosy sitting-room and her mother said: 'But I suppose you have your own flat lovely, you were always a great one for painting and decorating.'

Helen, relaxed with the flow of memories, did not reply with the clichés she'd been using ever since she came home but told her mother at length about the big free-and-easy apartment on the Amstel, its doors always open to anyone who needed help or shelter. She said they were trying to live their lives in love and simplicity and tolerance, and told how Caroline from the very day she was born had been encouraged to mix with people of all races and creeds and social levels without the slightest distinction. She described the economy of their lives, how she wove all the curtains herself and knitted or sewed every stitch they wore and how Pieter had retrieved some old dining chairs from the Flea Market and made them like new and how he constructed this massive table out of old beams from a demolished house – they needed a huge table, she said, for they never knew who or how many would descend on them at mealtimes. Her mother smiled and said yes, it sounds lovely, you seem to have no shortage of friends anyway, and then she changed the subject and said well it's getting near bedtime if we want to be up to catch this bus in the morning. Helen helped her to clear away the dishes and they went amicably to bed.

Miss Feeney arrived early next morning to take Caroline for the day and Helen, to hide her dislike of the old spinster, was effusive in her thanks. Miss Feeney looked at her sharply and said she used to put on less airs and graces and what were neighbours for, there was no need to make a ceremony out of it, and many's the time she'd looked after Helen aye and skelped her legs for her many's the time and the old ways were still the best and it was a poor thing indeed when young people grew too far away from the place and the people that reared them.

Well there's one that hasn't changed much, Helen thought, recalling how her mother had never been able to stand old Feeney either, and there they were now, apparently bosom friends, retired on the same day, identical bungalows a few yards apart, never done in and out making wee cups of tea for each other. Suddenly depressed she said: 'Ah sure we might as well take Caroline to Newry with us, there'll hardly be any danger,' but her mother said no, no it wouldn't be right to take the risk, especially after that ambush last night, two dead, it was on the News this morning, and Miss Feeney said you'd never forgive yourself Helen if anything happened to her and anyway Father Joseph's dying to have a good crack with her, a wee Dutch girl, he was out there you know in some Dutch colony for years and years, so Helen let her go and walked with her mother to catch the bus on the Square.

'Do you never get sick of old Feeney?' she asked, turning from the mountains she hadn't see for fifteen years to the road she hadn't seen either, its grass verges littered with rusty carcasses of burnt-out cars that even the soldiers were no longer fool enough to touch. 'Who? What's that?' Her mother had been dozing against the back of the seat and woke with a jerk. 'Feeney. She's a bit of an old pain, isn't she? How do you stick her next door?' 'Peg Feeney's a good neighbour to me, Helen, and she was a good principal for twenty years as well you know. I have nothing only the highest respect for her and never had.' 'Go away outa that with you!' Helen laughed. 'Sure you were never done complaining about her and making a joke of her as long as I remember, it's news to me she was a good boss to you.' 'When you get to my age, daughter, maybe you'll see the good of having someone nearby that you can depend on. When a body's own flesh and blood is not at hand –'

To Helen's relief she was interrupted; the bus was halted at a roadblock. 'The blaggards in green are the worst,' her mother whispered, 'Oul' RUC men!' Helen wasn't so sure: the young soldiers with their comically disguised faces looked nervous, their eyes skittering dangerously around and over the passengers. The others, the policemen, were older and solider; they might possibly act with thick brutality if they took the notion but were unlikely to fire off a shot out of pure panic. The soldiers took names and addresses. Two of their mates had died horribly the night before. Did they really believe the killers were casually sauntering to market on a quiet country bus? But then maybe they were. Helen gave her address in Amsterdam.

'What are you, a journalist?'

'No, I'm here on holiday.'

The officer laughed shortly: 'Christ, you must be a masochist! Actually I took the wife and kids to Holland last year. To the Keukenhof, been there?'

The kids and the flower festival and the pert little lacquered wife oohing and aahing over the pink flamingoes. Normality.

Sweet suburban decency and he must wonder, every time he put that clown's paint on his face, every time he manned a roadblock, if normality was something he'd seen the last of forever. Helen guessed he was seeing her as some link with a future in which he, lucky survivor, took the proud kids and adoring wife for a nostalgic dander through the tulip fields. She had an impulse to smile, to speak of the smell of hyacinths — because what unavoidable land-mine might he be already headed towards unbeknownst? — but she shook her head, cowardly, refusing friendly contact.

'Weren't they nervous!' she said, back in the bus. 'Did you notice their eyes?'

'Troth and I never look near them!' her mother answered loudly. 'I wouldn't give them that much satisfaction.'

A few people nearby murmured swift agreement, because who can you trust these days, and the murmurs caught and spread and rolled from seat to seat, ritual responses in a rosary of hate.

'Isn't it shocking,' her mother said when they were installed in a café halfway through the morning, 'Do you remember the time people could go here and there as free as they pleased? No roadblocks, no searching your handbag, and you weren't on the verge of a heart-attack every time someone left a parcel behind on a chair. Will it ever end, do you think? The pity of it, all this bombing and killing, God help us all, where will it finish up?'

'I thought you'd have been all in favour of it,' Helen said, to punish her for the scene on the bus. 'You were always so patriotic. It's a great thing to die for your country, you kept telling us from when we were no size. With Feeney it was die for your faith. You could say we had a choice all right!'

'This wasn't what I meant, nobody ever visualised this, Helen. Honest to God this brutality has little to do with patriotism, there's a difference between idealism and mindless killing, though I'm not saying they haven't a just cause. Only nobody ever recommended such –' Such blood, Helen thought, you imagined one could die for Ireland without blood and without vomit and without squeals, and above all without killing anyone else. A nice white smooth death, lying in one smiling photogenic piece under the green and saffron flag. But she didn't say it because what was the point of needlessly wounding? And her mother was after all just an innocent bystander: essentially good, essentially harmless.

'Did I ever tell you,' she asked instead, to lighten the atmosphere, 'about the time I tried to join the IRA? Well I was all of fourteen, it was the time Monica Quinn's mother took me and Monica up to Dublin for the weekend and Monica's brother, you know Jimmy, he was on the run for blowing up a Customs hut? Well I sort of saw me as the Countess Markiewicz and him as de Valera. I mean I was convinced he'd get me into the organisation, so Monica fixed up this rendezvous in the Phoenix Park and I went along trying to look about thirty all plastered in orange lipstick that I'd ripped off in Woolworths. So what happens? Along comes this great King Kong type, all beef. I mean I'd never met Jimmy before, and before you could say Patrick Pearse, he had me up against a tree and was trying to shove a hairy big paw down my dress! Imagine! So, I mean fourteen in that day and age, girls had a sex-age of about two, so I ran off screaming blue murder. But just think of it Mammy, only for that attempted grope your darling daughter would no doubt be making her own wee contribution to History!'

'No, you never told me,' her mother said. 'Well, we'd better be getting on. You have your shopping to do and I have a few things to get in the market.'

To Helen, walking through the grey town watching ordinary people with ordinary faces like her own smoking in quick nervous puffs up and down the pavement in and out of shops trying on synthetic jeans, buying packets of synthetic soup, their eyes sliding about at the floor, at the door, at the people beside and behind them, it seemed incredible that the danger they feared was real, that they were not dramatising themselves as she had been dramatising herself at fourteen, that the street could of a sudden burst open into flames and smoke and ruin, into a screech of disintegrating lives. That it had already done so several times. But it did not do so that day and they arrived home without incident. Miss Feeney brought Caroline back saying she'd been a great wee girl and no trouble at all. She refused the offer of tea and ran off home to cook a meal for Father Joseph who was a great eater.

'Look what I bought you in Newry, Caroline, and here Mammy this is for you, just a wee present.'

'Oh Helen you shouldn't have, the lovely scarf, ah sure it's too good to me you are, it's beautiful, Helen!'

'I thought it might go with that grey coat of yours, the one I got you in Paris, I see you still have it.'

'Which coat do you . . . Oh you mean that old grey thing in the wardrobe? Sure, daughter dear, that thing's in rags years ago! I never wear it now except an odd time I might throw it round my shoulders weeding. But Helen it wasn't you gave me that coat, that was an old one of Peg Feeney's, she gave me a whole lot of things, real good things, when she started to put on weight.'

'But Mammy no, the old memory must be going,' Helen laughed. 'Don't you remember the day we bought it, the awful row we had – I disgraced you in front of all the shopgirls going on about Che Guevara! Sure it has a Paris label and everything, you couldn't mistake it.'

'Well I don't remember it at all Helen, I honestly can't recall any row in a shop. Maybe you did buy me a coat, you were always too generous, but it certainly wasn't that one. I don't deny it has a Paris label because Peg bought it the time she went to Lourdes, oh seven years ago and then she got too stout for it and passed it on to me.'

Was that true? Could it be true and am I going mad, Helen wondered, trying to picture poor old Feeney trotting into the Saint Laurent boutique with her plastic shopping bag. There must surely be some mistake? But her mother was adamant – she could not remember Helen buying her a coat in Paris. She didn't need to throw it away, Helen thought bitterly, beginning to have an inkling. She threw me away instead, she just forgot about me for seven years, replaced me with old Feeney.

Then Caroline chimed in: 'Mum, do you know what Miss Feeney's brother did when you were in Newry? He washed my hair for me so he did.'

'What? What are you talking about? Washed your hair – of course he didn't wash your hair, stop telling fibs darling!' Everything's gone quite crazy, she thought with a giggle, seeing a tabloid headline: '*Elderly Priest Washes Little Girl's Hair.*'

'But he did Mum honest! He poured water on my hair and he said a recitation and he forgot the shampoo. And then Miss Feeney gave me sweets and she taught me the Name of the Father and the Angel of God.

Look Mum, want to see me do the Name of the Father for you?'

Helen understood. She turned on her mother in a fury. 'Do you hear that? She's away in the head your bloody old crony, she's halfway round the twist! And that creepy brother of hers, do you realise what they did? Fanatics, religious maniacs, my God, sure that's what they used to accuse old Paisley of long ago, inveigling children to his house to proselytise them. Christ mother I won't put up with this, I'll destroy the pair of them, I'll drag them through every court in the country, I'll –'

Her mother was standing there stiffly in front of her, as she had often stood stiffly and silently in front of an unruly class, wearing an expression Helen remembered all too well. They had jokes about it years ago – Helen used to say: Early Christian waiting for the cage to open. And Tim: Teetotaller about to refuse a drink at a Hunt Ball. Defiant and proud and brave, and slightly self-conscious.

'You knew about it mother, you put them up to it. How dare you, what right –'

'What right, what right! Hadn't I every right? My only daughter living like a slut with a man she's not married to, my only grandchild reared like a heathen. If you heard yourself, if you only heard yourself last night bumming and blowing out of you about the godless life you were leading, mixed up with drug addicts and communists and God knows what, letting your innocent child be corrupted by hooligans, ignorant trash of all creeds and colours. Did you expect me to sit up and do nothing? What class of a mother are you? Bragging to my face about how you stole from Woolworths when I was half-killing myself to give you a good education and the best of everything. You weren't worth my trouble, Helen, and that's something I found out long ago. I gave you every chance to mend your ways but you decided to go your own road. Well so be it, you made your choice, but don't expect me to stand by and do nothing when I see my only grandchild headed straight for Hell!'

And I thought she was changed, I thought she was harmless – seeing the straight simplicity of her mother's life, the ten commandments where they always were, eternal fire waiting for you if you broke them. She had a vision of what her own life must look like in comparison and for an insane second she wanted to fling herself in her mother's arms, cry: 'All right, all right I'll make a Catholic of her, I'll send her to Mass, I'll come home, I'll do anything you want!'

Instead she said coldly: 'Surely you mean Limbo, mother?' and went to her room to pack.

Tim drove her to Dublin early next morning: 'What possessed you to come crawling back? What were you expecting – the maternal lap shaken out of its mothballs for you, roses in the garden and your teddy bear waiting on the pillow? You're a bigger innocent than I thought!'

'Why did she send for me? She did send for me, Tim, was it just to have Caroline baptised?'

'Oh she thought she'd get you to stay, she's dead lonesome you know. After seven years she thought you'd have had enough of a life of sin and be ready to settle down and breathe the saintly air of Cross again. The savour of iniquity cloyeth on the tongue my dear brethren. Only you were no sooner arrived than it was Pieter this and Pieter that and the flat and the friends and the bloody windmills or whatever. She saw she hadn't a chance.

198

You didn't seriously imagine she was going to approve of you?'

'I thought she was changed, I dunno, slacker about things. But she *can't* have expected me to stay celibate, Christ I was only twenty-three when I split up with John!'

'And how old do you think *she* was when Daddy died? Do you think she ever looked at another man?'

'You disapprove too, don't you? You think I shouldn't have got married again?'

'Sure what do I care? You can't seriously believe your prolonged bout of adultery, or whatever you like to call it, is of any interest to anyone? In the light of all *this*?'

She followed his glance to the street of the border village they were driving through, its walls plastered with hand-written posters: DEATH TO TRAITORS! THATCHER OUT! KILL THE BRITS! Smudgy black photographs nailed to trees. Nothing had changed. Nothing ever would. She thought of her mother's letter and its nostalgic image of friendly fields, haws ripening on the bushes. What foolishness had possessed her, to return to this sick place? The hedges were black already, the leaves fallen, you could see the wind slashing wickedly across the famous landscape. Slane, Tara, an old grey monastery. Bogholes rich with the corpses of Cromwell's victims, preserved whole and intact after three centuries. Carrion scawl-crows sitting on posts waiting to gorge themselves on death and desolation. Big black crows rising off bare fences with a sudden meaningless shout of anger or boredom, flapping away aimlessly against the shabby sky. Black flags nailed grimly to tree-trunks: Pray for the soul of Bobby Sands. Pray for the soul of Raymond McCreesh. Pray for the soul of . . . Death was everywhere, it was in everything, and life was the unforgivable sin.

'There's places,' she said, with an impulse of charity towards this countryside she loved and hated and would not see again, 'I've lived in places where they think they can solve any problem under the sun by opening a mail-order catalogue or ringing up the relevant branch of the Social Security; do you think that's any better?'

'I do indeed,' he said seriously. 'I think it's a hell of a lot better. Wouldn't anyone in their senses?'

MICHAEL McLAVERTY

Mother and Daughter

T he old lady in the private ward had expected her married
daughter since two o'clock and since it was now nearing
four her scrap of patience had begun to shrink. Propped up in
bed with a woollen lavender cap on her head like a tea-cosy
she stared aggressively at the closed door and saw in its dull
glass panels the blurred figures of nurses passing to and from
the public ward. She could hear their bantering voices raised
in laughter and she grew more annoyed and tried not to listen
to them. They didn't give her much of their time, she reflected;
indeed, she could be dead and gone for hours before they'd
discover it. No one gave her a moment's notice, a moment's
consideration. She supposed private ward meant privacy – it
also meant neglect where she was concerned! And wasn't she
old, and wasn't she paying through the nose for this private
room, a room furnished like a Victorian hotel. And then there
was the bell-push looped round the rail of the bed which she
was to ring if she wanted anything. Oh, she liked that part of

it! How often had she rung and rung and no one had paid any heed to it. And it wasn't that the bell was out of order for the seldom time they did answer it they did so immediately.

But today you'd think they had gone on strike for she was sure she had a calloused finger from ringing the same bell. She was sure too her temperature and blood pressure were rising steadily.

She turned around and eyed the bell, and to appease her annoyance she pressed it again and heard it cheer itself hoarse in some part of the building. But no one answered it. Laughter came again from the public ward, and she wondered what they had to laugh at and maybe some poor patients needing a little rest or, God help them, lying at death's door. Come to think of it she herself would have been much better off in the public ward instead of being cooped up all alone like a Victorian dowager. For one thing she'd have had loads of company and loads of attention, and strange people traipsing in and out, and so many of them on visiting days there wouldn't be enough chairs for them to sit on and they'd have to perch on the edge of the bed or stand leaning over the bedrails. Her daughter wanted her to go there in the first instance and it was a pity she didn't heed her.

But what on earth was keeping her so late today after promising she'd be here at two. Oh, the same girl never hurried except when it suited her! Selfish, selfish – that summed her up.

She sighed resignedly and glanced at the chart hanging over the aluminum rail at the foot of the bed. She saw the black peaks and hollows on it like an outline of the Rockies and wondered what it all meant.

The door was knocked and a nurse slipped in.

'Did you ring, Mrs Collins?'

'On and off for the past three hours.'

'And what may I bring you or do for you?'

'You're all doing for me if you'd like to know! But I'll lodge a complaint to the doctor in the morning.'

'There are other patients in the hospital, too, Mrs Collins.'

'I don't want any impertinence, any back answers, either from you or anyone else. I'm in a private ward and I'm not paying dear money to be scolded or abused. All I ask is a little attention, a little consideration – half of what's given to the patients in the public ward would suffice.'

'We're doing our best for all, Mrs Collins. We're short-handed.'

'You may be short of hearing too, but you're not short-tongued. Would you please hand me my knitting from the top drawer there.'

'Let me prop you up on the pillows properly, and get you ready for your daughter.'

'I'll require that if she comes. What sort of a day is it outside?'

'It's snowing steadily and the roofs are covered white.'

'Snowing! Why wasn't I told so that I needn't expect my daughter. That's another instance of the silent cruelties of this place.'

'It only came on a short while ago.'

'You've an answer for everything, my girl. Perhaps you'd refill my hot water bottle before my poor feet are frozen stiff.'

'With pleasure, Mrs Collins,' and the nurse fished it out from under the bedclothes and held it in her arms as she would a baby. 'I'll be back in a minute,' and she smiled and hurried from the room.

Mrs Collins eyed the hand of the clock on the dressing table. She'd time that lassie.

Five minutes passed, and then ten.

She'd give her two minutes more before she'd poke the bell. Who ever heard of a quart of warm water taking ten minutes to boil!

I suppose she'll tell me the gas is on low pressure or the electric has failed because of the snow.

She lay back on the pillow and drew her feet up from the cold regions of the bed. She shivered. She'd get that blade to take her temperature when she'd come back! She stared at the clock and then gripped the bell-push and gave the button a prolonged squeeze.

At last someone stood outside the door and she could distinguish the white uniform of the nurse. She was talking to someone. Perhaps one of the young student doctors. The impudence of that one! The bottle would be cold by the time she had finished her tête-à-tête.

The door opened and the nurse came in backwards.

'I thought you'd never come and my poor feet frozen.'

'Was I long, Mrs Collins?' the nurse said brightly as she stowed the bottle beneath the blankets.

'It's a pity I'm not a young man and not an old woman. I'd get full value out of my private ward, I'm thinking.'

'You needn't expect your daughter today. By the look of it that snow's on for the whole evening.'

'Indeed I'll expect her! My daughter has a sense of duty. From an early age she was taught to have consideration for others.'

Mother and Daughter

'If your daughter's wise she'll stay at home,' and the nurse
stood at the window and gazed down at the snow obliterating
the cars tracks that led from the gate. 'I wouldn't be at all
surprised if the buses cease to run.'

'You're very comforting, I must say.'

'If you turn your head, Mrs Collins, you can see the snow
on the roofs. It must be an inch or so deep, for the outline
of the slates is blotted out.'

'If you give me the hand mirror I might be able to see the
snow without getting a crick in my neck.'

The nurse lifted the mirror from the dressing table, blew her
breath on it, and wiped it with the corner of her apron.

'Well now, Mrs Collins, what do you see?'

'I can see nothing except an old woman who's badly failed
since coming to this inhospitable place.'

'Indeed, you're looking well.'

'If you had seen me 20 years ago you would have seen
a very beautiful young woman. Anyone would tell you that
who knew me.'

'I'm sure.'

'The way you say it you're not so sure.'

'You're still handsome. One hasn't to go back 20 years to
find that out.'

'Why don't you sit down, nurse, and relax for a minute
or two.'

'You never saw a nurse sitting except at meal times. We're
always on the go.'

'If you are it's not to this room you do be going. It's little
attention I get from any of you.'

'If you needed attention we'd be in and out 20 times
an hour.'

205

'So I'm not sick at all – is that the next of it!'

'Oh, no, Mrs Collins,' the nurse smiled. 'You're still far from well. But you're no longer on our danger list.'

'If I were no longer on the paying list I'd be happy.'

The nurse rearranged a few bedraggled chrysanthemums in a vase at the window and on looking out saw Mrs Collins' daughter and grandchild coming through the gate.

'I must go now,' the nurse said without telling her the good news. 'Just ring if you want anything.'

Left alone the old lady lifted the mirror and watched the snow falling. Yes, the nurse was probably right. Her daughter wouldn't come, and that snow could be a convenient and plausible excuse. She lay back and shut her eyes, the hand mirror face downward on the eiderdown.

The door was knocked and in walked her married daughter with her six-year-old child. She carried a bunch of pink chrysanthemums that were moist with melted snow, and before greeting her mother she placed them upright in the wash basin.

'Are you asleep, Mother?' she whispered, stooping over the bed to kiss her.

'Sure you know I never sleep. And what possessed you to take Mary out with you on a day like this.'

She's in one of her tantrums, the daughter said to herself, and called on God to give her patience during the visit. Slowly she took off the child's cape and hat and draped them over the back of a chair, and sitting beside the bed she told her mother she looked greatly improved since her last visit.

'I may look it, Lizzie, but I don't feel it,' and thereupon she launched into a litany of complaints about the nurses' inattention and cold meals served up to her. The daughter sighed and patted the eiderdown, but after listening to another volley of complaints she said quietly, 'I wish, Mother, you weren't so querulous. The poor nurses are doing their very best.'

'Oh, if that's the mood you're in, my lady, you shouldn't have come out to see a sick and lonely old woman.'

'I don't like to hear you complain so much, that's all.'

'I'm not complaining, I'm just stating the bare facts.'

The child, not interested in their talk, wandered about the room, pulled out drawers in a bureau and was surprised that they contained nothing, only a blue sheet of paper flattened tightly to the bottom. Some of the drawers stuck as she was closing them, and one rather stubborn one she pushed so vigorously that a statuette of Our Lady rocked precariously on top of the bureau.

'Now see what you have done, Mary. Come here beside mother and keep your hands to yourself.'

'It's high time you corrected her. She's a little curiosity box.'

'Why do your teeth click, grandma, and mine don't?' the child said, staring at her grandmother and the lavender cap on her white head.

'What does the child say?' the old lady asked, leaning forward with a hand to her ear.

'She wants to know if you like her new blue cape.'

'She doesn't suit blue. You should have bought her a red one or a black one.'

The child, dashed, hid herself at the back of her mother's chair, but after a few minutes they had forgotten about her and she once more roamed about the room.

'John has a bit of a cold,' the daughter said, mentioning

her husband's name for the first time. 'But he'll be up to see you soon.'

'I suppose he's overworked these days,' the old lady said with false sweetness, aware that sloth was John's predominant passion.

The daughter clasped her hands on her lap and yearned to be out once more in the wide airy spaces of the street. No matter what she said she failed to make contact or break down the tension that divided them. Everything was going wrong: the snow, the long wait for the bus, and then the failure of the visit. She sighed, and as the daylight shrank from the room she switched on the light and drew the curtains.

And then suddenly there was a rumble and stumble on the floor, for the child had opened a press and out spilled bananas, turning black, and oranges and apples.

'Well, well, well, that's a spill! There's no peace with that child. Leave her at home next time you call.'

The mother stooped and pressed the burst bags of fruit into the press, and red in the face from exertion and anxiety she sat down and breathed audibly.

'You should give some of that fruit to the nurses. The bananas, I may tell you, are turning black.'

'They may turn pink for that matter. I wouldn't give the same nurses the skin of an orange if it were to save their lives.'

'The nurses! The nurses! Can you not stop pecking at them sometime. They're an overworked and underpaid body if you'd like to know.'

'That's right, stand up for them against your poor tortured old mother.'

The child by this time had discovered a small box of Turkish Delight that had fallen at the side of the press and she was poking a finger on the sugared jelly and licking it when her grandmother spotted her.

'My God, look what she has now!' she shouted. 'My Turkish Delight, the only sweet that lies at peace on my stomach. Hand them up this instant!'

She took the box and pushed it beneath her pillow, and the child, almost in tears, stood beside her mother and asked if they weren't going home soon.

'In a minute or two, Mary. Be patient, girly.'

'You should have left her at home instead of hauling her out through all that snow.'

'If I had left her at home you'd have asked why I didn't bring her. Oh, you haven't spoken a kind word to her since we came in.'

'I didn't wish to interrupt her plundering expeditions.'

'She didn't get much plunder as far as I can see!' the daughter flashed back, and then in an instant regretted it. The old lady closed her eyes, turned her head away, and raised a hand in a gesture of dismissal.

Quietly the daughter put on her own coat and then buttoned on the child's cape.

'Mother.'

'Let me sleep, please.'

She pulled on her gloves: 'Mother, I forgot to tell you that Sally Morgan is getting married.' She paused, but her mother didn't stir. 'She's getting married to . . . You'll never guess?'

The old lady shrugged her shoulders, but did not speak.

'We're going now,' her daughter went on. 'Is there anything special you want and I'll have it sent up to you?'

'Nothing, thanks. My needs are few. But do try to be in better form on your next visit.'

'I'll try, Mother,' she said, taking the blow. 'The snow and the long wait for the buses have put my nerves on edge, I suppose.' She stooped and kissed her mother.

The old lady looked fixedly at her: she wanted to ask her whom Sally Morgan was going to marry but she held back, stiffening herself against the impulse to please. But when the goodbyes were said and the door closed she felt her pride uncoiling in a long irregular line of angry discontent. She rang the bell. She wanted the nurse to call them back. She rang again and again but no one answered her.

Meanwhile her daughter had reached the outside gate, glad to be out in the free falling snow. She held Mary's hand tightly, but the child disengaged it, and while waiting for the bus watched the flakes turning her cape white.

They boarded the bus and the child knelt up on the seat, wiped the mist from the window with her gloved hand and looked out at the streets that were as white as the bed in the hospital.

'Why was grandma cross?' she asked.

'She wasn't cross, child. Your poor grandma is sick.'

'And what made her sick?'

'She's growing old.'

'And what made her old.'

'Turn round and sit on the seat like a good girl.'

The child turned around from the window and sat on the seat, watching the flakes of snow melt on her blue cape and dribble on to the floor.

At the centre of the city they had to change buses and stand in a queue. Beside them was a cafe and when the door opened the warm burnt smell of coffee rushed out into the cold air.

'Come, Mary,' the mother said, and taking the child's hand she led her into the cafe and sat at a round table near the window.

'And now, Mary, what would you like to eat?'

'Sweets, Mammy. Turkish Delight like grandma's.'

'We'll see.'

The mother rose from the table, crossed to the counter, and carried back two cups of tea, a few biscuits, and a small box of Turkish Delight.

The child smiled, took the box, and pushed the inside out like a matchbox. Lying closely side by side were cubes of coloured jellies dusted with fine sugar.

'You take one first, Mammy,' the child said.

The mother smiled, and to hide the warm tears of joy that rose up beyond her control, she lowered her head near the box and rhymed:

> Eena, meena, mina, mow,
> Catch a sweetie by the toe,
> If he squeals let him go,
> Out you must go.

She prised out a cube with her fingers and put it in her mouth. The child smiled, but seeing the tears in her mother's eyes she said:

'You're crying, Mammy.'

'The cold is making my eyes watery — that's all.'

'But it doesn't make my eyes watery,' she said, lifting out a sweet and putting it in her mouth. She smiled and looked at the large window that was misted over except for drops of water wriggling down the pane and leaving clear tracks behind them.

Is she thinking of her grandma and the hospital? the mother wondered, staring at her child.

The child swallowed the remains of her sweet and smiled:

'Look, Mammy, the window's crying. Look at all its tears.'

CAROLINE BLACKWOOD

How You Love Our Lady

F ather Callahan must be dead now – 'resting' – as he
always liked to call it somewhere in the mud of his own
churchyard. Maybe he is even still alive – maybe senile – and
living in some cottage with a housekeeper. 'O songless bird
far sweeter than the rose. And virgin as the Parish Priest. God
knows!' They all quoted then. Sometimes they used to quote
and counter-quote all through the night. I so loved to listen to
them, sitting next to Father Callahan in the wonderful light of
my mother's candles. They used to come to my mother's grey
Georgian house from Dublin – some of them even came from
further. My mother loved poets, painters and talkers. She said
she could only bear to be surrounded by 'free-spirits'. She
was always speaking about her love for Art and Nature, and
sometimes she said that she thought that life should be one
long search for the beautiful. My mother never made me go
to bed. She said that she detested the tyranny of the clock and
that all those who bowed to it were the poor trapped prisoners

of the temporal. Often in the mornings when I walked up to my convent through those grey, rock roads bordered by hawthorns, I felt so weightless and really weird from lack of sleep that it seemed to me that there was very little to stop me from floating up to the great white melancholy morning sky, and becoming part of it. And I would feel that I could understand why my mother often started repeating, when she was drinking in the evenings, that she thought that Life and Death were really the same – and both were beautiful.

I never liked my convent. Even Father Callahan could never really persuade me to like those nuns with their long, cold corridors punctuated by tormented, bleeding plaster Christs. Those nuns with their child-like skins, their canes and their crucifixes. I found the other convent girls so brutal, crude and frightening. They made the new girls hang their breasts over a towel-rail and then pricked them with safety-pins. Any girl who screamed they pricked much harder right on her nipples. I used to be so modest then – I remember that I cried while still only waiting for my turn, finding the mortification of being forced to stand half-naked in front of other girls almost as painful as the pricking. And long before they had drawn a drop of blood from me, I fainted. The Sisters were so cold, so fiercely disapproving, when I came to with ice-packs on my head in the sick-bay. They asked nothing – but I sensed that they could guess what had happened to me, and that like their own girls, they could feel only contempt for someone so frail – someone so completely lacking in the great qualities: courage, fortitude, self-sacrifice.

I learnt very little in my convent. I saw all my days as lost nights, and dawn only ever seemed to come to me when I was sitting after midnight, talking to Father Callahan in front of the heaped peat fires of my mother's drawing-room. I learnt only poetry to please my mother. Now I have forgotten almost all that I once knew. Who would want to listen to it now? My husband George slumped in his zombie stupor in front of the TV in our New York apartment? The elevator man? My coloured maid? It is strange but I still remember certain lines. 'A well dark-gleaming and of most translucent wave – images all the woven boughs above. And each depending leaf and every speck of azure sky . . .' My voice must have sounded so pure then. My mother would wipe her eyes when she heard it. She was always so proud of me when she saw me standing there reciting in my pretty white lace dress in the candle-light. In the evening when all her friends were there she would seem to feel a special warmth towards me and it would make her smile with delight if any of them said that I was like her. When we were alone together in the daytime I often felt a constraint, a nagging feeling of inadequacy as if I was perpetually failing her. Sometimes she made me feel like an egg that has been handpainted for Easter – an ordinary breakfast egg which shouldn't be fingered too much because all its gay dye can just come smudging off on the hand and then all its drab patches of everyday shell start to show. I knew that I had an underlay of drabness which distressed my mother far more than my occasional displays of insolence and disobedience. Whenever in her opinion I became commonplace she made it very clear that she only longed to get away from me, as if my dullness was like a disease that might contaminate her if she was too closely exposed to it. 'There is only one great crime', she would warn me. Her eyes would look almost blind as she spoke, as if they were filmed over with the glaucoma-like glaze of her own intensity.

'You can do what you like in this world. But you must always remember, Theresa, that the only great crime is to allow the humdrum to seep into your soul . . .' When she was in that kind of mood she nearly always started to talk about elms. She often said that you could get more education from just looking at trees and water than you could from wasting your days sitting on a hard bench in some nun-ridden soulless school. And then I would feel puzzled why she thought it necessary to send me to the convent. In any case elms were an obsession with her and she said they were the great tutors. 'Have you ever seen the way that an elm dies, Theresa? An elm doesn't die like other trees, you know. An elm dies from the inside. An elm dies in secret. You should always remember to be careful when you walk underneath elms for they can be dangerous. Elms are the only trees which give you no warning signs of their own decay. They can just come toppling down with a fearful crash while all their branches still look glorious and intact and all their leaves are still in bud. Once they are on the ground it can be quite frightening to see what has happened inside their trunks. Once they are dead you can see how the rot has eaten into them so hideously that they are completely hollow. People who allow themselves to become trivial and humdrum are like blighted elms. Eventually they are destroyed by being so filled with their own hollowness . . .' The more she would speak about dying elms, the more I would start to feel like one. Every thought that came into my head seemed like a threatening rot, it seemed to be so dull and dim and ordinary. Sometimes I feared that my mother had an X-ray power by which she could detect the banality of my unpromising thoughts and I pined to swallow some magic pill which would prevent me from ever boring her.

'You have misnamed your daughter,' my mother's friends would tell her after they had listened to me reciting in the evenings. 'The child is no Theresa. She is a Deirdre. Just look at that face! And the girl is ready for her Naisi – but now all our Deirdres are doomed to be guarded by nuns who are far fiercer and more deadly than any jealous old King Concubar!' – 'That child is not human,' they would keep repeating. 'She is one of the Sidhe!' The Sidhe – the enchanted spirit race of ancient Ireland. 'God fuck you!' they shouted at my mother, 'you are repeating the tragedy of the country. You give birth to a Sighoge – and you allow its lovely spirit to be mutilated in a bleeding convent!' They would lift up their glasses in a toast to me and then tip their wines and whiskeys on to my mother's carpet. They smashed their glasses down on the floor and ground them to a sugary powder with their heels. They shouted things like 'Long live the Fenian men!' and 'Up the I.R.A.!' My mother would laugh and go to play her piano. Father Callahan would take my hand. I would feel his palms which were as cool, smooth and unused as those of a young child. He always took my hand when they started to blaspheme. Often when the wine was on them they would hurl blasphemies back and forth across the room like delinquents throwing stones. I was often frightened that some dreadful flaming retribution would strike and smash the whole house. But then when Father Callahan took my hand I felt comforted, thinking that his very presence under our roof must act as some kind of talisman with the power to ward off the scourge of the Divine Anger. 'Never be disturbed by blasphemy,' he would whisper to me. 'Blasphemy is only the lining of the coat of Belief. Blasphemy is only the lining turned inside out.'

He must have been a very young man then, Father Callahan.

It is hard for me even now to realise it. At the time he seemed like the bleak, beautiful hills that I could see from my mother's window, even older and sadder than Christianity. He drank, Father Callahan. This always rather surprised me. He drank solemnly, treating his wine as though it was a sacrament. And his drinking seemed to increase not only his sadness, but also his sobriety. My mother always served special vintage whiskeys and brandies and very good French wines. She said that she could only tolerate the 'excellent' – that a true love of quality was a 'Life Caring'. She collected old blue Waterford glass and had very good plates on her dresser. She wore only beautiful laces and wine-coloured velvets. She said that she had to live beside water, that her blood came from the sea, and she claimed as an ancestor some fierce Spanish sailor who had been smashed up on the Galway rocks from the Armada. Outside her house a waterfall crashed through the night. Everyone had to shout in her drawing-room. They shouted against the cascade of water that fermented and foamed like angry beer as it hit the rocks. They shouted against the crash of my mother's piano. My mother always played very loud. She knew so many songs. All the new English songs, and the laments of the old Gaels. Her voice could sound as thunderous as any man's, and while she played and sang, her face flushed scarlet, her huge eyes flashed and rolled in her head, her great breasts heaved up and down so violently that they seemed about to break through her wonderful velvet dresses, and her long hair streamed down over her shoulders, ink-black from perspiration. Often as the night went on she seemed enchanted, almost demented by her own music. And frequently by the time that morning started to break on the hills it seemed as though her piano was really playing her –

and she was only its exhausted instrument. And many times when she stopped her playing, she would fall like a stone to the ground.

'Your mother is a nymph!' Father Callahan once said to me. 'She is surely the very same nymph that sucked Finn down into the waters. It is no wonder that he stayed so long down there that his hair had turned white by the time that he came up again!' I think he knew how much it always pleased her when anyone said rather exaggerated and high-flown things like that.

I wonder if I ever really properly understood the way that Father Callahan loved my mother. I always felt that his love for her was very different from the love of all the poets and drinkers and talkers who came every night to her drawing-room and so often ended up in the 'Doss-House' as they called her spare room where rows of mattresses were always laid out on the floor for anyone who felt like staying. I thought then that Father Callahan's love for my mother was mystical – almost abstract – like his love of the blood of the Martyrs – like his worship of the Saints. I felt that there was pain in his love and some deep reconciliation to loss. Whatever Father Callahan really felt for my mother, I was only glad at that time that it seemed to extend to me as my mother's daughter. He spoke only to me in the evenings. Father Callahan never seemed able to interest my mother. She would smile at him sometimes when she was sitting at her piano. But then when she was playing she quite often smiled at anyone who happened to be sitting around drinking in her drawing-room. She smiled, but it was as though she did not really see them. She certainly very rarely took the trouble to come over to address one word to him, and I often wondered why she kept on inviting him.

She told me once that to dream about priests was very bad – that even if you dreamt about the Devil, it was much, much better. She also said that she hoped that I would never accept any gift from Father Callahan – even if it was something as small as a halfpenny or a handkerchief – for any gift from a priest could bring the most atrocious bad luck. 'And that's about all we need,' she said.

'What do you mean?' I asked her.

'When you are older,' she answered, staring out through the window to the waterfall, 'you will start to find out that very many things – can have very many meanings.'

'Shall I get you a cup of tea?' I asked her. I always disliked it when she started to speak in riddles. And she seemed so restless that day, unable even to settle down to her piano. I saw the disgust in her eyes and I knew that I had disappointed her. 'Yes,' she snapped at me, 'I suppose that you really might as well do just that!'

'You live too much in the past, Theresa,' my husband very often tells me. I wonder if I do. And I wonder if George notices where I really live, just so long as he can still see me sitting in my chair in his expensive West Side apartment. More and more I feel like that crusader that as a child I always hated so – that repulsive little Irish crusader who lay in his open coffin and had his hand shaken by tourists in the vaults of St Michan's in Dublin. 'It is one of the miracles what has preserved him here without embalmment!' the guide was always saying. And surely some guide seeing me sitting with George in our living-room could very well say the same about me now. My mother so loved those terrible musty vaults of St Michan's. She said that they still contained the lovely spirit of Parnell because he had once been laid out in state there. Sometimes she would take me down to visit them as often as three times a week. 'Shake the crusader's hand for luck, Theresa!' And I still remember the feel of his hand – so cold – so smooth – so shiny: the feel of a well-soaped saddle. 'As you see, the human nail continues growing after death,' the guide would keep on pattering. Those dreadful nails! The nails of a society woman – but so much yellower and almost as long as the chicken-bone fingers they were sprouting out of. Sometimes my mother said that she wished my father could have been buried under the church of St Michan's. 'He would have been with us still.' And I was always guiltily glad that she had never got her wish. I remember that the lights once fused when I was down in those tombs with my mother. We were forced to stand there in the darkness for nearly an hour while the guide, who was always stocious drunk, stumbled around cursing while he tried to find the fuse-box. My mother never stopped screaming. She said that she had felt the crusader brush her spine with his finger-nail. All the same the next week she was saying it was always beautiful to shake the hand of History. And very soon we were both back down there again.

'It seems to me that it really was your own lights that fused when you were down in those goddam tombs with your mother!' George sometimes says to me. 'It's sick, Theresa! It's really sick the way you live so much in the past!' But often while I potter round his apartment in the daytime, and often in the evenings while I sit watching him as he watches his favourite Late-Late Show while he files his toe-nails with his nail-file, I do not feel that I live in the past. Like that dismal little crusader I still have a hand which anyone can shake if they feel inclined to – but quite frequently I feel that I do not really live at all.

'You ought to see an analyst, Theresa. You reject everything. It's as if you feel that nothing can ever be so miraculous as all the old times that you spent with your screwy nut-case of a mother and her bunch of provincial Irish bullshit artists. You are utterly out of touch with reality. You really seem to live in some kind of a crazy Celtic twilight . . .' I listen very attentively to all my husband's criticism. Now I may very well live in some kind of a twilight. But in a Celtic one? That I wonder . . . George often has a curious imprecision when it comes to using words. I watch George sitting with his head in his hands while he tries to think up some advertising slogan for sanitary-towels. 'Soft – Soft – Thistle-down Soft! Eliminates all fear of those tell-tale bulges!' 'It's beautiful George! It really has quite an amazing lyrical freshness!' 'I don't need any of your boring patronage, Theresa. Look, you are a woman – you ought to know about sanitary-towels. Don't just sit there acting so goddam superior. For Christ's sake just try for once and give me a little bit of help!' I look at him sitting there paralysed like some great podgy slow-witted schoolboy who has got hopelessly stuck in his lessons. 'Have you thought about Baby-bottom Soft, George? Maybe that would be even better than Thistle-down.' He considers it. And for one moment we are almost quite close. We suddenly have a bond. We are suddenly a team. But then George shakes his head. 'One thing I'll say for you, Theresa. You are certainly never the slightest fucking help.'

'Feeling sorry for yourself is your only full-time profession!' that poet of the sanitary-towel sometimes shouts at me. 'How you love yourself, Theresa – just yourself – and only really ever yourself!' 'How you love Our Lady!' my mother said to me one night when I was sitting talking to Father Callahan in her drawing-room. She rolled her huge beautiful eyes so scornfully down his long black trailing skirts and then she laughed really maliciously. 'I wonder,' she said, 'just how long you will be able to keep that up!' Father Callahan never seemed to hear her when she spoke like that, although the blood crept out from behind his ears and trickled down towards his nose like some slow advancing army. And soon she was back at her piano and had forgotten him. 'O Boyne, once famed for battles, sport and conflicts, And great heroes of the race of Conn,' she would moan, 'Art thou grey after all thy blooms? O aged woman of grey-green pools, O wretched Boyne of many tears!' Father Callahan would sit beside me and stare into her fire with his sad bloodshot eyes and speak to me of life, and death, and the nature of humility and evil, and of the Divine Perfections. Quite often he would say that all he prayed for me was that when I was a little older I would still have the strength to remain 'white'. 'White? What is white?' I would ask him, although I knew well enough from the girls of my convent, and I only wanted to hear him explain it. 'You will know, my daughter. You will know in your time,' he always answered me, pouring himself another brandy. Sometimes he would start to speak so intensely that I really could not follow what he was saying, and frequently his soft voice was completely wiped out by all the clash of glasses, and bottles and opinions, and the thunderous wail of my mother's singing, but often, while he was speaking to me and I kept drinking her excellent red French wine, Father Callahan's dark clerical clothes started to look brighter to me than all the brilliant silks and velvets of my mother's friends, and I felt that it was of no importance that he was a priest, and that I was a child, for we were like two disembodied spirits who had found such perfect harmony that it was impossible for anything ever to break it – and therefore nothing again could ever make me feel afraid.

Sometimes my mother would suddenly jump up from her piano and start screaming at all her guests. She would tell them that they were all just a gaggle of geese-like fools. She said she felt she would die unless she breathed some fresh air, and could hear the sound of water. And then she would grab Paddy Devlin or any other man who was still able to stand by the hand and drag him out through the door and take him down to the waterfall. Father Callahan always became very agitated when she behaved like this, although none of her other guests seemed to take much offence at her insults. Indeed a lot of them were usually sprawling half-asleep on the carpet at the time, or else locked away in some of the lavatories vomiting, and I doubt that they remembered all her abuse by morning. But Father Callahan always became very tense and miserable. He never seemed to be able to concentrate on conversation while my mother was out somewhere lost in the darkness. Often she would stay outdoors for what seemed like hours, and the whole time Father Callahan would never stop flicking his eyes towards the door, like a dog that keeps waiting for the return of its master. Once when my mother had stayed out even longer than usual, Father Callahan suddenly started quoting to me for no particular reason from his favourite Cardinal Newman. 'The Catholic Church holds it better for the sun and moon to drop from Heaven, for the earth to fail and for all the many millions on it to die of starvation in extremest agony, as far as temporal affliction goes, than that one soul, I will not say shall be lost, but should commit one single venial sin . . .' 'And where is the Charity in that, Father?'

I asked him. 'There are very many enigmas,' he answered me irritably.

Were Father Callahan's enigmas all theological? Even now I feel that there are still so many questions. Even now I still keep asking myself – why did I never guess at that time – why did I never for one moment guess that there was something so elm-blighted, and most certainly enigmatical, behind all my mother's singing, and her quoting, and her over-hectic pagan laughter?

Father Callahan and Doctor Donovan were standing side by side in her drawing-room when I got back one day from my convent. The doctor was a very tall man, and seeing the priest standing beside him in his long dark trailing skirts, I remember thinking that Doctor Donovan looked rather like a bridegroom, and Father Callahan like his small black bride. Their faces looked strange – rigid – almost angry – and the sight of them made me feel afraid.

'Daughter, have courage.'

'What has happened?'

'Daughter, pray for strength. Remember it is only an ante-chamber.'

'What is only an ante-chamber, Father?' My heart was pounding. I thought for a moment that he was speaking of my mother's drawing-room.

'Life,' Father Callahan said slowly. 'Life, as you know, is only really just an ante-chamber to Eternity.'

'Has something happened to my mother?' I turned to the doctor. He was so silent. I saw his eyes flick nervously to Father Callahan. Why should he not answer me? He was such an old man. He was such a tall man. He was a doctor. Why could he not answer me without waiting for the priest?

'It's all over with her,' Father Callahan said. He looked different to me in the daylight. His face looked suddenly weak and blotchy – rather ordinary and unintelligent, like the faces of so many of the ill-nourished adolescents that always hung around the bar-tents at all the races. 'Let us kneel.' Father Callahan dropped down on his knees on my mother's drink-stained carpet and the doctor copied him a little awkwardly with his long stiff thighs. I remained standing. I remember staring at the curtains of the drawing-room. I had never noticed before that their scarlet velvet was so shabby. They were drooping down from their poles like limp, faded washing.

'Were you there, Father Callahan?' I asked him.

'I was.'

'Did she see you come.'

'She did indeed. The Lord was very merciful. She was conscious for nearly one hour.'

'But that is really terrible! She must have known why you had come!'

'She knew, of course.'

'But how could you have done that to her, Father Callahan? She must have hated to know. She must have been so absolutely terrified to know!'

'She wanted to know. But in any case she would have had to know. How could she be allowed to go in her sins?'

'But I don't understand how your mind worked, Father Callahan. I know that you never liked to face it – but you know just as well as I that she was never a believer. She despised priests. She despised what she called their doggerel. What use did you think you could be to someone like that? She must have felt a total panic at the very sight of you arriving so horribly final and chilling in your black. Maybe she still had a little hope until she saw you. I wish that you had never let me know the terrible thing that you did to her. Oh, why couldn't you have just kept away from her?'

'I tell you my child that when she saw me, she was glad. My presence in her agony was a consolation. It is to them all.'

'But maybe she wouldn't have needed any consolation, Father Callahan, not if you had never made her know only too well why you had come.'

'You are speaking quite wildly, my child. It is your grief. You still know absolutely nothing of the facts.'

'But I know how much she hated to know anything unpleasant, Father Callahan. She was someone who cried if other people trod on wild flowers. She was never in the least bit brave. Is that not true, Doctor Donovan? You remember that she was even terrified of injections. She could never bear to know when they were coming. She always stuck her arm out as far as it would go – and she turned her head away – and squeezed her eyes tight shut. The way she would scream and moan – it was really quite horrible to hear it – and always long before the needle had even gone into her!'

'My child, you seem quite demented. You are speaking of things which are quite beside the point.'

'You knew her, Father Callahan!' I started crying. 'You came to our house every evening. You knew what she was like. You loved her. You know very well that she would have wanted to go like an animal – like a butterfly – knowing nothing. Even if she had no chance – why couldn't you have allowed her to go on still believing that she had some tiny chance? I know that her hopes must have been hopeless. But what right did you have to take those last little hopes away from

227

her? I will never understand how you had the cruelty to do that to her!'

'Don't speak disrespectfully to the Father!' Doctor Donovan suddenly snapped at me from his kneeling position on the carpet.

'She is not railing at me. She is only railing at me as the vessel of something so much higher that it passes her comprehension.' Father Callahan looked exhausted and the blotches on his face were becoming so brilliant that they resembled a disease.

'I tell you, my child, that she was serene. When it finally came to her, there was very little struggle. The end is often not at all like you imagine. It is often somewhat of an anti-climax.'

'An anti-climax!' I saw him shiver as I screamed at him. 'For you it may have well seemed like an anti-climax, Father Callahan. But I hardly think that it could have seemed very much like that to her. She was not a priest you know, Father Callahan. She loved all sorts of things. She loved love – she loved water – she loved poetry – she loved music. She was someone who loved life!'

'She can't have loved life as much as you imagine.' Father Callahan bent his head in prayer. 'May the Lord have mercy on her.'

'What makes you say that?'

'It was horrible . . . But she couldn't be blamed. Something must have entered into her. She wasn't herself. She just turned on herself. She died of her wounds. She grabbed a carving-knife. Her real self can't have been with her. It was plain at the end that she never intended it. She was the one that sent for Doctor Donovan. He did all that could be done for her. But she had been too savage . . .'

HARRIET O'CARROLL

Trust

When Juliet Culhane was born, it was decided among all who knew the family that she would be a source of inconsolable grief. It was agreed between friends and relatives alike that it was the greatest pity that this last and unexpected child, this uncalled-for and uninvited bonus, should turn out instead to be a burden and a blight.

The consultant who delivered her felt that his money was hard-earned when it involved him in interviews such as the one he held with Mrs Culhane. In the small green room, surrounded by the scent of congratulatory flowers, he tried to muffle in clinical phrases the stark and unpalatable facts of the baby's future. Mrs Culhane was no fool, and through the technical verbiage she acknowledged the truth with terror. The baby was maimed, had been even before her birth. She was damaged, physically and mentally, beyond hope of recovery. Her life would be short. She might not speak, she might not walk, no one could say. Mrs Culhane fixed her eyes on the buttons of the doctor's waistcoat and hoped the tears would not come.

'It's a genetic condition,' the consultant said. 'It's not as yet understood. Fortunately it's very rare. You must think of it as a matter of bad luck. It's no one's fault, no one is responsible. As yet we don't understand these things well enough to be able to avoid them.'

Why me? Mrs Culhane thought, why me and mine?

She tried to think of the questions she should ask and found only the useless and unanswerable 'why' thundering in her brain. And behind each why another why hovered, equally insistent, equally useless.

She could see that he was anxious to be gone. There was no more she wanted to hear from him. Composedly, she said 'I see' and 'thank you' and 'good-day', and listened to his footsteps, departing, she imagined, to the free air of the golf course and the trivial preoccupation of his handicap.

The traffic ground along in the street outside, and the dust danced in the sunbeams. She suffered wave upon wave of grief. She suffered for herself and four others. With flinching pain she thought of her three older children, of how she would tell them and of how they would take this blow. She thought of her husband, first with a sort of agony at what she had to tell him, then gradually with some consolation and relief. He would cope with this as he had coped with other trials in their life together. They would share it and it would not shatter them. That much at least was sure in the whirlpool of misery around her.

She felt an immense weariness, and thought that if she could sleep for a month she might wake up with the energy to deal with the problems to hand. She tried to summon the

230

words she would use to tell Dick about the baby, but her mind went around in circles. With softness and pity, she thought of the baby. She got out of bed and walked over to look at her. Juliet looked tiny, neat and self-contained, like a sea creature in a protected pool. It was hard to believe she would always be as vulnerable as she was now, that she would grow only in size. She got back into bed and drifted into a half-sleep.

She dozed through the twilight till the darkness came and the white fluorescent wands were flicked on in the corridor outside. Dick wakened her as he opened the door. She had no words prepared, no tones of consolation, no saving graces to offer. Yet she did not make too bad a job of it. She knew him of old and how he liked to be approached. Bad news could not be wrapped up. 'Get it out and get it over,' he used to say to the children.

'Dick, there's something wrong with the baby. She won't grow up, and she won't grow old. It's something she was born with, a syndrome of some sort they call it. There's no cure.'

He walked over to the window and drummed his clenched fist gently against the pane. She wanted to touch him but there was a thousand miles between them. 'This is a bitch of a thing to have happened. But what about you? Are you all right yourself?' Dick never used strong language.

Then they held each other, and went over the whys and the maybes, and tried to imagine their future with their sad, doomed baby.

The reactions of their friends and relations was the first trial. So many thought to console Mrs Culhane by telling her stories worse than her own. She could not see how her own misery should be relieved by comparing it with the unhappinesses of others. But she held her peace and allowed them to ramble on.

Mrs Culhane had forgotten the biological pull exercised by a baby – her next youngest child was twelve years old. Juliet was a quiet infant, ominously quiet when she thought about it. She often approached the cot in fear, listening hard for the rustle of tiny breathing. Dick was gentle with the baby; he had always been good with children. At times he stared at Juliet in puzzlement, as if unable to believe that her fate had been so finally decreed.

Someone suggested she should join an association for parents of handicapped children. At the first meeting she found that she had opened a Pandora's box of emotions. She was disturbed by the sad, ineffectual anger she met again and again. This rage was directed at helper and adversary alike, it was a hopeless tearing at the fates, a revenge for inexplicable punishment. Then she met the saddened but surviving few, and wondered how they had achieved such acceptance. When she came away from these meetings, she was often harassed, unwillingly confronted by a world of difficulties. Occasionally, she was heartened by the camaraderie of misfortune. She consoled herself with the knowledge that the rest of the family had taken their tragedy with a matter-of-fact equanimity. They got on with their lives, and she did the same as best she could.

A social worker called to tell her that if she found it impossible to cope, she could put the child on a waiting list for a residential home. 'It might be better to put her name on the list in case you need a break. It's not easy to get into these places, especially the best ones.'

'I should be able to manage,' Mrs Culhane said. 'She hasn't got much, has she? She might as well have me.'

And all the time, Juliet was there, like a partial eclipse, a permanent shadow on their daily living. She was a duty, a worry, and then gradually against all inclination, a small joy. When she was about eight months old, Mrs Culhane could no longer resist the knowledge that the baby was gently responding to her. She felt pain she had not felt before – she was being asked to open her heart to love and to loss. Who could ask her to love when she must give up so soon? And yet how could she deny this helpless, stupid being who had nothing in life but trust?

Mrs Culhane became acutely miserable, so that the rest of the family could not reach her. She stared glumly at Juliet for an hour at a time. She cancelled bridge games and craft classes to sit at home, as if paralysed. Dick tried to persuade her to go out, assuring her that he would mind Juliet. The teenage children hovered around the gloomy creature their mother had become.

It was a trite popular song that broke her mood. She was peeling potatoes by the kitchen window when the words from the radio penetrated:

> We'll sing in the sunshine,
> We'll laugh come what may,
> We'll play in the sunshine
> Then you'll go on your way.

Tears flowed and fell into the peelings in the sink. Between crying and smiling she prayed the only prayer she had ever prayed for herself and Juliet. She prayed that she could find it within herself to enjoy today's happiness without thinking about tomorrow, that she would let go without bitterness when the time came. She prayed that the few years she would have with Juliet would be spent in the present and that when Juliet was gone the past would be left behind.

It was too much to hope for, of course. Nevertheless, the shell of fear cracked and she began to let herself notice the baby's budding personality. Juliet's eyes followed her when she moved. At first Mrs Culhane thought it coincidence. Still, those blue unfocused marbles swivelled in her direction time and time again. Despite her obvious imperfections, her flaccid limbs and asymetric shape, Juliet had the vulnerable appeal of all babies. Wrapped and dressed, only her eerie, wizened face could be seen, but floating in the bath, her subtle surfaces, her dreamy pearly curves, had lovable perfection. Released by the warm water into something approaching perfection, Juliet's belly undulated among the water drops. Small sensations flitted on her stolid face. What did it matter if she relapsed into impassivity when she was dried and dressed? Count the credits, forget the loss.

Juliet also began to develop likes and dislikes. Mrs Culhane introduced her to the experience of taking food from a spoon. Mashed pears, bananas, and drops of honey were acceptable; minced meat and carrots were not. Such parallels with normality were delightful. Juliet was admitted into the family routine so that her presence was no longer an eclipse. Her obvious preference for her own family, they took as a compliment to their competence. They enjoyed seeing in her what others could not, as if they had learned the language of an extinct tribe and were the only ones qualified to communicate.

'That child,' said Dick without rancour, 'has us all trained like robots. It takes me half an hour of talking to get the same response she gets with one grunt.'

'It's not what you grunt, it's the way that you grunt it,' replied the eldest. 'You don't expect us to listen to you, Dad. You might ask us to do something. Or even give us advice. But Julie baby, she just wants the dribble wiped off her chin or to be moved into the sun.'

Mrs Culhane had begun to realise that on a scale of relativities she was lucky. At her meetings she discovered that she could have had to contend with a much more disastrous situation. Juliet did not scream for hours on end. She did not bang her head against the wall and disfigure herself with great black bruises. Neighbours and family could sleep, undisturbed by frantic howling.

By the time Juliet was four she was able to sit up and shuffle around on her bottom. The social worker rarely called and when she did she was usually the recipient rather than the dispenser of sympathy.

'No air in my tyres again when I came out of the flats this week. I do wish they'd discriminate between intending friend and foe.'

'I don't know how you do it,' said Mrs Culhane.

'Nor I you, Mrs Culhane. That was a lovely cup of tea. You're a bright spot in a dismal day. Goodbye for now. Bye, Juliet.'

Then Juliet's health began to slide. The first infection did not much disturb any of them – a child with a temperature was not an unusual thing. Then the relapses came fast upon each other. Juliet ill was a more common state than Juliet well. With the onset of every illness Mrs Culhane inwardly pleaded, 'Not yet, not yet. I am not ready.' Their doctor suggested that the baby be admitted to hospital. The parting was like a preamble to death. Mrs Culhane hated walking those ungiving hospital tiles, she hated what she saw as Juliet's diminishment into a case and a condition. More than anything else, she hated the sense of exclusion she felt. She swore that if Juliet were sick again she would let her live or die at home in peace and dignity. Even as she swore she knew that her treacherous mix of love and fear would send her flying for the help of hospital and medicine again. Then as Juliet's temperature stopped swinging and her breathing became deeper and more even, the hospital became a different place. The division and threat melted away.

There was a photograph of Juliet in the kitchen. It had been taken one sultry August Sunday when the grasshoppers were chirruping in the back garden. Mrs Culhane looked at the image, dull eyes and floating fish-like limbs, and said joyously, 'Three more days and you'll be home.'

As she came home with Juliet she did not believe that trees could be so green nor square paving stones so pretty in the sudden rain as they then seemed. Their days continued as before, but with a sense of waiting. Juliet survived that winter and in the summer she lay on a rug in the garden and waved her fingers at the sun. She chuckled at the flicking leaves and smiled when garden insects marched across her legs.

She died the following winter, as they had known she might. It was a loss they could only share with each other. They thought how pitiful it was that she should have died having sampled so little of life. They listened to words of condolence and knew that their friends and relatives saw the death as a relief. But they had loved Juliet, and in her five short years they had not come to the end of their patience or their affection. Other people did not know what it was like to live in the glow of her unresented trust. They had learned the language of her slight demands, they had coaxed her silences into laughter. Mrs Culhane felt that she grieved doubly for Juliet, for there were so few to grieve.

They drove home from the graveyard. They walked together into the empty house where the baby's photograph smiled at them from the kitchen shelf. Mrs Culhane took off her coat and went to fill the kettle.

'I'll never be able to forget her,' she said.

'No,' said Dick, 'you won't forget her but the pain will pass. You know you did everything you could.'

They made the tea and sat around the kitchen table. They spoke about Juliet, embalming her in their memories, mentioning only the happy times. Already they were beginning to accept her death as they had accepted her life. She had lived without reflecting and had died without knowing. And they had made that short space into a period of gentleness, an episode of trust, a time when they had been measured and found not wanting.

LIAM O'FLAHERTY

The Cow's Death

The calf was still-born. It came from the womb tail first. When its red, unwieldy body dropped on the greensward it was dead. It lay with its head doubled about its neck in a clammy mass. The men stood about it and shook their heads in silence. The wife of the peasant who owned the cow sighed and said, 'It is God's will.' The cow moaned, mad with the pain of birth. Then she wheeled around cumbersomely, her hoofs driving into the soft earth beneath the weight of her body. She stooped over the calf and moaned, again smelling it. Then she licked the still body with her coarse tongue lovingly. The woman rubbed the cow's matted forehead, and there was a tear in her eye; for she too was a mother.

Then the cow, overcome once more with the pain, moved away from the calf and stood with her head bent low, breathing heavily through her nostrils. The breath came in long pale columns, like sunbeams coming through the window of a darkened church. They drove her away to a corner of the

238

field, and she stood wearily with her head over the fence, lashing her flanks with her tail restlessly.

They seized the calf and dragged it by the feet along the field to the fence, out through the fence into another field, then through another fence, then up the grassy slope that led to the edge of the cliff. They dropped it downwards into the sea. It lay in a pulped mass on the rocks. They rebuilt the gaps in the stone fences carefully and returned to the cow. The woman offered her a hot drink of oatmeal, but she refused it. They seized her and poured the drink down her throat, using a bull's horn as a funnel. The cow half swallowed the drink, half tossed it away with her champing mouth.

Then they went home, the woman still moaning the dead calf and apologising to God for her sorrow. The peasant remained with the cow, watching until she should drop the bag. He buried it under a mound of stones. He dug his heel in the ground, and, taking a handful of the brown earth, he made the sign of the cross on the cow's side. Then he too went home.

For a long time the cow stood leaning over the fence, until the pain lessened. She turned around suddenly and lowed and tossed her head. She took a short run forward, the muscles of her legs creaking like new boots. She stopped again, seeing nothing about her in the field. Then she began to run around by the fence, putting her head over it here and there, lowing. She found nothing. Nothing answered her call. She became wilder as the sense of her loss became clearer to her consciousness. Her eyes became red around the rims and fierce like a bull's. She began to smell around on the ground, half running, half walking, stumbling clumsily among the tummocks of grass.

There was where she had lain in travail, on the side of a

little slope, the grass compressed and faded by the weight of her body. There was where she had given birth, the ground trampled by many feet and torn here and there, with the brown earth showing through. Then she smelt where the calf had lain. There were wet stains on the grass. She looked around her fiercely, and then she put her nose to the ground and started to follow the trail where they had dragged the calf to the fence. At the fence she stopped and smelt a long time, wondering with her stupid brain whither the trail led. And then stupidly she pressed with her great bulk against the fence. The stones cut her breast, but she pressed harder in terror and the fence fell before her. She stumbled through the gap and cut her left thigh near the udder. She did not heed the pain, but pressed forward, smelling the trail and snorting.

Faster she went, and now and again she raised her head and lowed – a long, mournful low that ended in a fierce *crescendo* – like a squall of wind coming around a corner. At the second fence she paused again. Again she pressed against it, and again it fell before her. Going through the gap she got caught, and in the struggle to get through she cut both her sides along the flanks. The blood trickled through jaggedly, discolouring the white streak on the left flank.

She came at a run up the grassy slope to the cliff. She shuddered and jerked aside when she suddenly saw the sea and heard it rumbling distantly below – the waves seething on the rocks and the sea birds calling dismally with their noisome cackle. She smelt the air in wonder. Then she slowly advanced, inch by inch, trembling. When she reached the summit, where the grass ended in a gravel belt that dropped down to the sheer slope of rock, she rushed backwards, and circled around wildly, lowing. Again she came up, and planting her feet carefully on the gravel, she looked down. The trail of her calf ended there. She could follow it no further. It was lost in the emptiness beyond that gravel ledge. She tried to smell the air, but nothing reached her nostrils but the salt smell of the sea. She moaned and her sides heaved with the outrush of her breath. Then she looked down, straining out her neck. She saw the body of her calf on the rocks below.

She uttered a joyful cry and ran backwards, seeking a path to descend. Up and down the summit of the cliff she went, smelling here and there, looking out over the edge, going on her knees and looking down and finding nowhere a path that led to the object on the rocks below. She came back again, her hind legs clashing as she ran, to the point where the body had been dropped over the precipice.

She strained out and tapped with her fore hoof, scratching the gravel and trying to descend, but there was nothing upon which she could place her feet – just a sheer drop of one hundred feet of cliff and her calf lay on the rocks below.

She stood stupidly looking at it a long time, without moving a muscle. Then she lowed, calling to her calf, but no answer came. She saw the water coming in with the tide, circling around the calf on the rocks. She lowed again, warning it. Wave after wave came in, eddying around the body. She lowed again and tossed her head wildly as if she wanted to buffet the waves with her horns.

And then a great wave came towering in, and catching up the calf on its crest swept it from the rocks.

And the cow, uttering a loud bellow, jumped headlong down.

Acknowledgements

IVY BANNISTER: 'My Mother's Daughter', reprinted from *Prize-Winning Radio Stories* (Mercier Press) by permission of the author.

MARY BECKETT: 'Under Control', reprinted from *A Literary Woman* (Bloomsbury) by permission of the author.

CLARE BOYLAN: 'The Little Madonna', reprinted from *Concerning Virgins* (Penguin Books) by permission of the author c/o Rogers, Coleridge & White Ltd., 20 Powis Mews, London W11 1JN.

HELEN LUCY BURKE: 'A Season for Mothers', reprinted from *A Season for Mothers* (Poolbeg Press) by permission of the author.

BRIEGE DUFFAUD: 'Innocent Bystanders', reprinted from *Nothing Like Beirut* (Poolbeg Press) by permission of the author.

Acknowledgements

MARY LAVIN: 'Senility', reprinted from *The Shrine* (Constable) by permission of the executors of the author's estate.

MARY LELAND: 'The Little Galloway Girls', reprinted from *The Little Galloway Girls* (Hamish Hamilton) by permission of the author.

BERNARD MacLAVERTY: 'In Bed', Copyright © Bernard MacLaverty, 1994, reprinted from *Walking the Dog and other stories* (Cape) by permission of the author c/o Rogers, Coleridge & White Ltd., 20 Powis Mews, London W11 1JN.

MICHAEL McLAVERTY: 'Mother and Daughter', reprinted from *Collected Short Stories* (Poolbeg Press) by permission of the executor of his literary estate.

VAL MULKERNS: 'Summer', reprinted from *Antiquities* (André Deutsch) by permission of the author.

EDNA O'BRIEN: 'Cords', reprinted from *The Love Object* (Jonathan Cape) by permission of the author and the Wylie Agency.

HARRIET O'CARROLL: 'Trust', reprinted from *Blackstaff Short Stories 1* (Blackstaff Press) by permission of the author.

MARY O'DONNELL: 'Scavengers', reprinted from *Strong Pagans and other stories* (Poolbeg Press) by permission of the author.

Acknowledgements

JULIA O'FAOLAIN: 'Lots of Ghastlies' Copyright © Julia O'Faolain, 1974, reprinted from *Man in the Cellar* (Faber) by permission of the author c/o Rogers, Coleridge & White Ltd., 20 Powis Mews, London W11 1JN.

LIAM O'FLAHERTY: 'The Cow's Death', reprinted from *The Short Stories of Liam O'Flaherty* (Cape) on behalf of Liam O'Flaherty Copyright © 1937, 1948, by permission of the Peters Fraser and Dunlop Group Ltd.

While every effort has been made to trace all copyright holders, the publishers would be glad to hear from any who may have been omitted.

Biographical Notes

IVY BANNISTER: Born New York, she has lived in Ireland since 1970. She has published a collection of short stories, has won a Hennessy 'New Irish Writing' Award and the Mobil Playwrighting Ireland Award, and her plays and stories have been performed, published and broadcast in Ireland, England, Germany and the USA.

MARY BECKETT: Born Belfast, she moved to Dublin in 1956. In the early fifties her stories appeared in *The Bell*, *Threshold* and *Irish Writing*, but the preoccupations of raising a family prevented her writing again until 1979, when her story, 'A Belfast Woman', was published in *New Irish Writing* and became the title-story of her first collection. Her much-praised novel, *Give Them Stones*, was published by Bloomsbury in 1987, followed by her second story collection, *A Literary Woman*.

Biographical Notes

CAROLINE BLACKWOOD: Born Co.Down, 1931, she lived for some time in England and America and was married to the poet, Robert Lowell. She published novels and short-story collections, and also wrote on cookery, gastronomy and wine. She died in 1997.

CLARE BOYLAN: Born Dublin, 1958, she won the Benson & Hedges Award for outstanding work in journalism before turning to full-time creative writing in the early eighties. Her widely acclaimed debut novel, *Holy Pictures*, has been followed by three more, and she has also published three story collections, essays on fiction writing, and *The Literary Companion to Cats*.

HELEN LUCY BURKE: Born Dublin. A winner of the PEN Short Story Award, she has published a short-story collection and a novel. In recent years she has become one of Dublin's leading commentators on the capital's restaurants.

BRIEGE DUFFAUD: Born Crossmaglen, N. Ireland, 1941, she spent most of her adult life in London, Amsterdam, and the South of France, where she now lives. She has won a Hennessy 'New Irish Writing' Award, and has published a novel and a collection of short stories.

MARY LAVIN: Born in the USA, 1912, she was brought to Ireland when she was nine. Educated at the Loreto Convent and University College, Dublin, she became one of the great short-story writers of the century with a world-wide reputation, winning many awards and two Guggenheim Fellowships. She died in 1996.

Biographical Notes

MARY LELAND: Born Cork, where she still lives. She first worked on the *Cork Examiner*, then as a Production Assistant with RTE, and is now a writer and freelance journalist. She has published two novels and a collection of short stories.

BERNARD MacLAVERTY: Born Belfast, 1945, he went to live in Scotland and won an award from the Scottish Arts Council for his first collection of short stories. He has since published three further collections and three novels, the latest of which, *Grace Notes*, won the Whitbread Novel Award.

MICHAEL McLAVERTY: Born Co.Monaghan, 1907, he was a graduate of Queen's University, Belfast. A mathematics teacher, he wrote eight novels and many short stories which established him as one of Ireland's leading writers. He died in 1992.

VAL MULKERNS: Born Dublin, 1925, she published her first short stories in *The Bell*. A member of the Irish Academy of Letters, she has published three story collections and four novels, and in 1984 was awarded The Allied Irish Banks Prize for literature.

EDNA O'BRIEN: Born Co.Clare, 1930. Love in all its forms has been the dominant theme of her many novels and short stories since her celebrated debut novel, *The Country Girls*, in 1960. For many years she has lived in London, and her writing has won her international acclaim.

HARRIET O'CARROLL: Born Callan, Co.Kilkenny, 1941. She has won a number of short-story competitions as

247

well as being joint winner of the O.Z. Whitehead 1988 Playwrighting Award. Her work has also been broadcast by the BBC and RTE.

MARY O'DONNELL: Born Monaghan, 1954. A graduate in German and Philosophy, she worked for some years as a translator in Heidelberg University. Her early poems and stories appeared in The Irish Press *New Irish Writing* in the eighties, and since then she has published two novels and three poetry collections.

JULIA O'FAOLAIN: Born Dublin, 1932, she was educated at UCD, Rome and Paris. One of Ireland's most distinguished writers, she has published two story collections and five novels.

LIAM O'FLAHERTY: Born Inishmore, the largest of the three Aran Islands, 1896, he won a scholarship to UCD, but left after a year to join the Irish Guards. He fought at the Somme and on the Republican side in the Irish Civil War. His wide literary reputation rests on his short stories, of which he wrote over one hundred, but he also wrote fifteen novels, one of which, *The Informer*, became a classic Hollywood film. He died in 1984.